What's black, crispy, and sits on top of the roof?

An Irish electrician.

●

Hear about Snow White's swingin' party?

She woke up feeling Dopey.

●

What's the purpose of a belly button?

It's a place to put your gum in on the way down.

●

What's worse than your dentist telling you you have herpes?

Your mother telling you.

**TURN THE PAGE FOR MORE
OUTRAGEOUSLY TASTELESS JOKES**

OUTRAGEOUSLY TASTELESS JOKES

Blanche Knott

ARROW BOOKS

Arrow Books Limited
17-21 Conway Street, London W1P 6JD

An imprint of the Hutchinson Publishing Group

London Melbourne Sydney Auckland
Johannesburg and agencies throughout
the world

First published in Great Britain 1985

© Blanche Knott 1984

Compiled and adapted from
Truly Tasteless Jokes IV
and
Truly Tasteless Jokes V
by Blanche Knott,
originally published in the USA by Pinnacle Books

Set in Lectura type by
Photobooks (Bristol) Ltd

Printed and bound in Great Britain by
Anchor Brendon Limited, Tiptree, Essex

ISBN 0 09 944450 X

Contents

Ethnic Variegated   7
Irish   17
Handicapped   26
Celebrities   30
Cruelty to Animals   34
Male Anatomy   45
Female Anatomy   60
Homosexuals   72
Religious   79
Child Abuse   88
Old Age   90
Miscellaneous   96

Ethnic Variegated

How can you tell when you're at an Australian stag party?

A sheep jumps out of the cake.

•

What's dumber than four Italians trying to build a house underwater?

Six Poles trying to lay the foundation.

•

What do you call an Armenian with lots of girl friends?

A shepherd.

•

Did you hear about the Italian who thought a vulva was an automobile from Sweden?

•

What do the Chinese call 69?

Two Can Chew.

•

What do you call birth-control pills in Italy?

Wop stoppers.

•

Did you hear about the West Indian burglar whom the cops swore they could hear a mile away?

He finally got wise and left his radio at home.

●

What's this?

●

A Mexican riding a bike.

●

What's this?

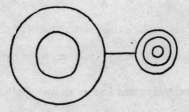

A Mexican frying an egg.

●

What's this?

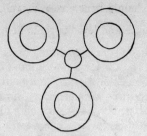

Three Mexicans pissing in a can.

●

What do blacks and Christmas trees have in common?
They both have coloured balls.

●

Who was the first black prostitute?
Kunta Kinte's sister – Rentacunta.

●

What goes black-pink-black-pink-black-pink?
A black jerking off.

●

What does the Jewish Santa Claus say as he comes down the chimney?
'Ho-ho-ho! Anybody want to buy some toys?'

●

Mr Cohn, Mr Katz and Mr Rabinowitz are such avid golfers that their wives finally get fed up with being 'golf widows' and insist on a two-week vacation in Miami Beach. On pain of divorce, each promises not to even mention golf to his wife. But by the third day all three are climbing the walls, and sure enough where do they run into each other on the fourth day but the local golf course. 'You wouldn't believe this, fellows,' moans Cohn, 'but this game is costing me $45,000 for a new Mercedes for my wife.'

'You think that's bad,' says Katz, 'listen to this: I've got to shell out $110,000 for a new condominium.'

Rabinowitz smiles and says, 'You poor schmucks, I'm here without it costing me a penny. At six a.m. I rolled over and said, "Well, Becky, what's it going to be, golf course or intercourse?" She says, "Take a sweater so you don't catch cold."'

●

A woman goes into a Jewish delicatessen and buys two loaves of raisin bread. About an hour later the phone starts ringing; the owner of the deli answers it and it's the lady shopper. 'Listen,' she hisses into the phone, 'the raisin bread I bought from you has two cockroaches in it! Now, what are you going to do about it?'

The deli owner thinks it over, then replies, 'Bring back the cockroaches, and I'll give you two raisins.'

●

Did you hear about the sequel to *Jaws* about a loan shark?

It's called *Jews*.

●

A young New York Jewish man takes his mother to a film about life in ancient Rome. She's from the old country and has a little difficulty following the customs in this strange land, so at one point she asks her son to explain a scene in progress. 'This particular scene,' he whispers, 'shows how in those days the Romans often persecuted the Christians by throwing them in the arena to be devoured by lions.'

Studying the gory image for a few moments, she points her finger at a lion in the far corner and shouts, 'And dat vun – vy isn't he eating?'

10

●

Her daughter the anthropologist has been off in darkest Africa for fourteen months and has just announced her engagement to the man of her dreams. So the Jewish mother is almost beside herself with excitement when they arrive at the airport for a holiday. Seeing her daughter come through the gate accompanied by a huge black man with a bone through his nose, clad only in a grass skirt and bead necklace, for a moment she is struck speechless. Then she sobs, 'Oh, Rachel, I wanted for you a rich doctor, not a witch doctor!'

●

What's a Jewish porno film?

Ten minutes of sex, fifty minutes of guilt.

●

What do you call a picnic in Madrid?

A spicnic.

●

An American Pole was so proud of his new red Cadillac that he just had to show it off, so he cruised through the black part of town. At a traffic light a black giant hauled him out of the driver's seat, drew a circle around him in the road, and told him not to step out of the circle unless he wanted to get the shit beaten out of him.

The black guy started to demolish the Cadillac, starting with the headlights and windows, when he heard the Pole laughing. He moved on to the body and engine, but in between crashes he could still hear the Pole's hysterical giggles. Finally the black guy came over with his crowbar and said, 'What in hell you laughin' at? Your fancy car's never gonna run again.'

Snickering, the Pole replied, 'So? Ever since you've been tearing up my car, I've been stepping in and out of this circle.'

11

What do you get when you cross a Mexican with a faggot?

A señor-eater.

•

I have good news and bad news:

The bad news is that the Martians have landed in Carlisle, and they eat human babies.

The good news is that they're headed north.

•

Hear about the Great Wall of China?

It has chinks in it.

•

This is the story of the Italian who went to visit the USA:

One day I'ma go to a bigga hotel in Detroit. I goa down toa breakfast and say to da waitress, 'I want two piss of toast.' She only branga me one piss, so I say, 'Heya, waitress, I wanta two piss.' She say to go to the men's room. I say, 'You no understand, I wanta two piss on da plate.' She say 'You better not piss on the plate, you sonna ma bitch!' And I don't even know her!

Later I goa toa lunch atta Drake Restaurant. The waitress branga me a spoon anna knife but no fock, so I say, 'Heya, waitress, I wanna fock.' She say everybody wanna fock. I say, 'You no understand, I wanna fock on the table.' She say, 'You better not fock on the table, you sonna ma bitch!' And I don't even know da lady!

Later I goa toa my room, but there's only one sheet on da bed. I tell da manager, 'I want two sheet,' and he tells me to go to da toilet. When I explain, he say, 'You better not shit on the bed, you sonna ma bitch!'

Finally I goa toa checkout. Ima leavin' and da man at da desk say, 'Peace to you.' I say, 'Piss on you too, you sonna ma bitch! I go back to Italy!'

The wealthy Iranian tourist was outraged at being searched by Customs on his arrival at JFK Airport. 'New York is the asshole of the world!' he screamed.

'Yessir,' said the customs official. 'Are you just passing through?'

•

A Frenchman, an American and a Pole are going on a drive through the countryside when their car breaks down. A few miles down the road they come across a farm and are offered shelter for the night. Showing them to a room, the farmer says, 'Just don't stick your dicks in those three holes.'

But horniness and curiosity overwhelm the visitors in the middle of the night; the Frenchman sticks his dick in the first hole, the American in the second, and the Pole in the third.

'Okay, wise guys, who used the holes?' asks the farmer the next morning.

'The first one was *magnifique*,' exclaims the Frenchman. 'What was eet?'

'My wife's pussy,' says the farmer.

The American confessed to the second, saying how nice and tight it had been. 'That's good,' says the farmer. 'That was my daughter's pussy.'

The Pole, whose dick is all bandaged up, says, 'The third hole was great, but after a while it began to hurt like hell. What was it?'

The farmer says, 'A milking machine that doesn't stop till it gets five quarts.'

•

How do you confuse a Polish road worker?

Give him two shovels and tell him to take his pick.

•

What do you get when you cross a Mexican and a Spaniard?

Spic 'n Span.

●

An Englishman was enjoying his vacation in Sicily when he came across a roadblock manned by an armed bandit. Ordering him out of his rent-a-car, the bandit commanded him to masturbate. 'I can think of worse fates,' thought the tourist as he dutifully obeyed. The bandit told him to do it again and the tourist complied, though this time it took a little longer. 'Again,' commanded the Sicilian, ignoring his victim's protests and waving his gun around, and the fellow finally managed to jerk off a third time.

'Okay,' said the bandit. 'Now-a my sister ride with you to town.'

●

What do Italian mothers do when their children misbehave?

They wop them.

●

What do you call Japanese cunnilingus?

Constluctive cliticism.

●

What do you call a genetic engineering company in Italy?

Genitalia.

●

What do you get when you cross the Texas Chainsaw Massacre with a group of Eskimos?

Cold cuts.

●

Did you hear about the new Italian steel-belted radial tyres?

Dago forward, dago backwards and when dago flat, dago wop, wop, wop, wop.

●

An Englishman, a Scotsman and a Chinaman were working in the coalmines. The Englishman was in charge of digging, the Scotsman was in charge of shovelling, and the Chinaman was responsible for supplies.

The Englishman discovered he needed some more tools, so he sent the Chinaman to go and get them. Two hours later, the Chinaman hadn't returned so the other two went looking for him. As they rounded a corner in the mine shaft, the Chinaman jumped out from behind a pillar and yelled, 'SUPPLIES!'

●

Who killed more Indians than Custer?

Union Carbide.

●

A Texan and a Pole were transporting several prize cows aboard a twin-engined plane. When one of the engines sputtered and died and the plane began to tilt, the Pole commented, 'If that other engine goes, we're gonna crash.'

Sure enough, a minute later the second engine gave out. In a panic the Pole shouted, 'What're we gonna do? We're going down.'

'Don't worry,' said the Texan calmly.

'Don't worry! What about your family?'

'Don't have any,' said the Texan.

'What about the cows?'

'Fuck the cows!'

'Gee,' said the Pole, 'have we got time for that?'

●

Did you hear how the dumb Swede flunked his driver's test?

He opened the door to let out the clutch.

●

Did you hear about the new Japanese-Jewish restaurant?

It's called So-Sue-Mi.

Irish

An Irishman was jumped on by two muggers and fought like hell, but he was finally subdued. His attackers went through his pockets. 'You mean you fought like that for fifty-seven pence?' asked one of the muggers incredulously.

'That's all you wanted?' moaned the Irishman. 'I thought you were after the two hundred pounds in my shoe.'

●

What black, crispy, and sits on top of the roof?

An Irish electrician.

●

Three Irishmen go out on the town, looking for a good time. The first loses no time in picking up a pretty brunette and they disappear off to her place. The second soon finds a willing redhead and they check into a hotel across the street. The third eyes an attractive blonde and asks if she wants to come back to his flat and have a wild time. 'I'd love to,' she says, 'but I'm on my menstrual cycle.'

'That's quite all right,' said the Irishman. 'I rode my moped.'

●

An Irishwoman went into the chemist's and asked for a deodorant for her husband. 'Certainly,' said the sales assistant. 'How about the ball type?'

'Oh, no,' she said, 'it's for under his arms.'

What did the Irishman say when he stuck his head into the toilet bowl?

'Howdy, doody.'

Why did the Irish couple decide to have only four children?

Because they read in the newspaper that one out of every five babies born in the world today is Chinese.

Why did eighteen Irishmen get together to go to the same movie?

Because they read the sign UNDER SEVENTEEN NOT ADMITTED.

Did you hear about the Irish girl who had two chances to get pregnant?

She blew both of them.

An Englishman, an Irishman and a Welshman all hear about a legendary bridge: if you have the courage to jump off it, and the presence of mind to shout in midair what you want to become, your wish will be granted. So they make the trek to the bridge and the Englishman says he'll be daring and jump first. Over he goes, yells 'Billionaire!' and lands safely on the deckchair of his giant yacht. The Welshman jumps next, shouts 'An eagle!' and soars up into the heavens. The Irishman runs for the edge, stubs his toe on the kerb as he jumps, and yells 'Oh, shit!'

Why don't Irishmen play hide and seek?

Because nobody will go and look for them.

●

Hear about the Irishman who thought cross-breeding was getting a little on the side?

●

Secretary: 'May I use your Dictaphone?'

Irish boss: 'Use your finger like everyone else.'

●

Why did the old Irish lady have her tubes tied?

So she wouldn't have any more grandchildren.

●

Why didn't the Irishman want to buy any pornographic materials?

The needle on his pornograph was broken.

●

An Irishman was wandering through London when a prostitute sidled up to him and purred, 'Baby, if you have ten pounds, I've got the time.'

'Thanks,' said the Irishman, 'but I already have a watch.'

●

Did you hear about the Irish bulletproof vest?

You get your money back if it doesn't work right.

●

It's time for an Irishman's regular medical check-up and the first order of business is being weighed. Feeling self-conscious about his weight, he asks if he can take off his sweater. Then, holding it carefully away from him in one hand, he steps back on the scale.

The pilot and co-pilot of a transcontinental flight are conversing in the cockpit when the co-pilot notices one of the four jet engines catching fire. 'Hey, Bob, how are we going to cope with this?' he asks a bit nervously.

'No problem. Listen.' The pilot picks up the microphone and announces, 'Attention, all passengers: This flight will be twenty minutes late.'

Ten minutes later, engine two quits. 'Attention, all passengers: We will be forty-five minutes late.'

Pretty soon engine three conks out. 'Attention, all passengers: We will be an hour and a half late.'

Two Irishmen in economy class look at each other and one says, 'If that last engine goes out, we'll be up here all day.'

●

Two Irishmen emigrated to America. On their first day off the boat in New York they spied their first hot-dog vendor in the street. 'Do they eat dogs in America?' one asked his companion.

'I don't know.'

'Well, we're going to live in America, so we must learn to do as they do.' So they each bought a hot dog wrapped up in wax paper and sat down to eat them on a nearby park bench. One Irishman looked inside his wax paper, then over at the other Irishman, and asked, 'What part did you get?'

●

Heard of the new Irish invention?

It's a solar-powered flashlight.

●

An Irishman, a German and a Frenchman were driving across the country when their car broke down. They asked a nearby farmer if they could sleep in his barn. The farmer grudgingly agreed, but said, 'You'd better be quiet, though. I don't like prowlers, and I'm likely to shoot first and ask questions later.' The three men agreed not to make any noise and lay down to sleep, but eventually the Frenchman had to get up and take a leak. As he stumbled down the stairs in the dark, he heard the farmer cock his rifle and shout, 'Who's that?'

'Meow,' said the Frenchman, and the farmer went back to bed.

A little while later the German too felt the call of nature, but again a 'Meow' calmed the jumpy farmer.

When it was the Irishman's turn he got as far as the foot of the stairs before the farmer called out, 'Who the hell's *that?*'

Said the Irishman, 'It's me, the cat.'

●

An Irishman came home early from work to find his wife lying on the bed, panting and sweaty. 'Honey, I think I'm having a heart attack,' she gasped. The Irishman ran downstairs to call the doctor, and on the way his little son told him, 'Daddy, daddy, there's a naked man in the wardrobe.'

The Irishman ran back upstairs, opened the wardrobe door, pulled out his best friend, and yelled, 'Jesus, Jack, Mary's having a heart attack, and here you are, scaring the kids!'

●

Did you hear about the Irishman who was found unconscious in his jail cell with twelve bumps on his head?

He tried to hang himself with a rubber band.

●

Why shouldn't you buy Irish goldfish?

They drown.

●

Did you hear about the Irish gynaecologist who used two fingers?

He wanted a second opinion.

●

How can you tell an Irishman from an ape?

The ape peels the banana before eating it.

●

What do you call a stork who brings Irish babies?

A dope peddler.

●

Two Dubliners decided to try out country living so they bought a farm complete with all the livestock. The first thing they did was to make sure all the animals were properly housed. They put the dog in the kennel, the chickens in the coop, the pigs in the sty, and the cows in the barn. Everything went smoothly until they reached the door of the mule's stall – the animal's ears kept hitting the top of the doorway and, like any self-respecting mule, he refused to go a step further.

After talking the problem over, the two Irishmen decided to jack up the side of the barn and walk the mule into his stall. They had the barn raised up about three inches when a tourist happened by to ask for directions. Seeing what they were doing, he suggested they dig a ditch instead, and walk the mule into his stall.

'Now isn't that typical?' said one Irishman to the other. 'Any fool can see it's the mule's ears that're too long, not his legs.'

●

An Irishman was working at a construction site where the boss left each day at 11.00 a.m. and was gone for two hours. This became such a regular occurrence that the rest of the workers decided to spend the two hours in the bar across the street, but the Irishman decided to head home for some extra nookie with his wife. When he arrived home, he found his boss busy banging his wife in the bedroom! Well, he walked straight out and headed back to the job.

The following day the Irishman was slaving away when everyone headed across to the bar. 'Hey, Seamus, aren't you coming?' asked one of them.

'Hell, no,' said the Irishman.. 'I almost got caught yesterday!'

●

What does an Irishman write on a postcard?

'Hi. Having a great time. Where am I?'

●

This Irish odd-job man was going from door to door in a suburban neighbourhood seeing if there was work to be done. An older man answered the doorbell and said that, yes, in fact the porch badly needed repainting. They agreed on a price and the Irishman was furnished with paint and a brush and shown to the back of the house.

The man was quite pleased when the Irishman came back in after only two hours and reported the job done. Commenting on the Irishman's fast work, he paid him the money and let him out the door. The Irishman thanked him and said, 'And by the way, that's not a Porsche, that's a Mercedes.'

●

How many Irishmen does it take to start a car?

Five. One to steer, one to work the pedals, two to push, and one to sit under the hood saying, 'VaROOM, VaROOM.'

●

An Irish couple and a single man are shipwrecked on a desert island. It doesn't take long for the single man to feel pretty horny, and finally he comes up with an idea for getting into the wife's pants. Climbing up a tall palm tree he hollers back down to the couple, 'Hey, you two, quit fucking down there!' The Irishman looks over at his wife – who's standing ten feet away – and says, 'What the hell's he talking about?'

This goes on for several hours, until the married man is overcome with curiosity and decides to climb up the palm to see for himself what the other man's problem is. As he's going up, the horny fellow jumps down to the beach, grabs the wife, and proceeds to screw her like crazy.

The Irishman finally reaches the top where the single man had been, looks down, and says, 'Begorrah, if he wasn't right – it does look like they're fucking down there!'

●

How about the Irish girl whose boyfriend said he loved her?

She believed him.

●

How do you stop an Irish Army amphibious landing?

Shoot their rubber horses.

●

How do you tell an Irish ladder from a normal one?

The Irish one has the word 'STOP' stencilled on the top rung.

●

An Irishman is walking down the street and passes a hardware store advertising a cut-price sale on a chainsaw that is capable of cutting 700 trees in seven hours. The Irishman thinks that's a good deal and decides to buy one.

The next day, he comes back with the saw and complains to the salesman that the thing didn't come close to cutting down the 700 trees the advert said it would.

'Well,' said the salesman, 'let's test it out at the back.'

Finding a log, the salesman pulls the starter cord and the saw makes a great roaring sound.

'What's that noise?' asks the Irishman.

●

Paddy and Mick rent a private plane for the day and are doing fine until it's time for touchdown. Paddy is busy with all the instrument readings and finally gets the plane down, but has to screech to a stop. 'Boy, that's a short runway,' he says, wiping his forehead.

'Yes,' agrees Mick, 'but look how wide it is.'

●

Handicapped

A man had been going to a psychiatrist for many years, and finally the doctor pronounced him cured of his mental illness. On hearing the news, the ex-patient smiled, shook the doctor's hand, and pulled out a revolver.

'*What the hell are you doing?*' screamed the shrink.

'Well, doctor, you've helped me a hell of a lot . . . but now you know too much!'

•

Where do epileptics go when in Las Vegas?

Seizures Palace.

•

Did you hear about Martha the midget?

She went into the bar and kissed everyone in the joint.

•

How about the amputee with cancer?

He had one stump in the grave.

•

How do crazy people go through the forest?

They take the psycho path.

•

Bumper sticker: *Roses are red,*
Violets are blue;
I'm schizophrenic.
And so am I.

●

Did you hear about the one-legged lady who got raped?

She couldn't cross her legs to save her ass.

●

What do you call a man with no arms or legs in the postbox?

Bill.

The same man in a spice-rack?

Herb. Or Basil.

The same man covered with oil?

Derek.

The same man, who always gets shat on?

Lou.

What do you call a girl with no arms and no legs going down a river?

Flo.

The same girl on a fence?

Barb.

Okay, what do you call a man with no arms or legs halfway down Tina Turner's throat?

Mike.

What do you call two men with no arms or legs hanging on a wall?

Kurt 'n' Rod.

What do you call a man with no arms and legs and with a speech impediment in the sink?

Dwayne.

And what do you call a quadruple amputee with a scratched-up face?

Claude.

●

What's the difference between Quasimodo and a messy room?

You can straighten up a messy room.

●

What's the definition of agony?

A one-armed man hanging off the edge of a cliff with an attack of crotch itch.

●

Doctor (taking up his stethoscope): 'Big breaths.'

Patient: 'Yeth, and I'm not even thixteen.'

●

What do you call a midget fortune-teller who escapes from prison?

A small medium at large.

●

How do you make a Venetian blind?

Poke him in the eye.

●

Did you hear about the fellow with two wooden legs?

He caught fire and burnt to the ground.

●

What is a leper's favourite rock-and-roll song?
Footloose.

●

Why is it illegal to tell jokes in a leper colony?
They might laugh their heads off.

●

How can you tell when a leper has been in your shower?
Your bar of soap has grown.

●

Celebrities

Who killed David Kennedy?

Syringe Syringe.

•

What the difference between Elizabeth Taylor and a Guernsey cow?

Fifteen pounds and eight husbands.

•

Why did Alex Haley try to commit suicide?

He found out he was adopted.

•

What has three balls and comes from outer space?

E.T.— the Extra Testicle.

•

What were the last words Marvin Gaye's father said to him?

'This is the last 45 you'll ever hear.'

•

How did Marvin Gaye die?

He heard it through the carbine.

•

Heard about the new Detroit record label?

It's called 'Mowdown'.

●

What do a Crunchie bar, Kentucky Fried Chicken and Michael Jackson have in common?

They're all dark and crispy.

●

Hear about the new shampoo Michael Jackson's endorsing?

It's called Head & Smoulders.

●

What's the name of Michael Jackson's new album?

Griller.

●

What do you call it when Dolly Parton does the backstroke?

Islands in the Stream.

●

What has 500 pounds of hair and can't get through a revolving door?

Dolly Parton.

●

One day Boy George got some good news and some bad news. The bad news was that his girlfriend had left him. The good news was that all her dresses fitted him.

●

Why are the Democrats consulting with Jane Wyman?

Because she knows how to screw Reagan and then dump him.

•

What's Roman Polanski's latest movie?
Close Encounters with the Third Grade.

•

What's John Lennon doing these days?
Decomposing.

•

How did Dolly Parton get two black eyes?
She went jogging and forgot to wear a bra.

•

How about why David Kennedy was buried at sea?
So Uncle Ted could drive to the funeral.

•

What was John Lennon's last hit?
The pavement.

•

If Castro were gay, what would you call his lover?
An infidel.

•

What do Richard Pryor, Michael Jackson and Hot Lips
Hoolihan have in common?
Major burns.

•

What kind of birth control does Spock use?
A vulcanized rubber.

•

What's the difference between Darth Vader's prick and his laser sword?

His prick gets hard and hot when *he* gets turned on.

●

What do the Ayatollah Khomeini's buddies think of him?

They all think he's a hot shiite.

●

Did you hear they're building an archive for the Nixon papers?

No admission charge—but you have to break in.

●

Cruelty to Animals

An Irish biology professor was conducting research on the nervous system of the frog. Taking a frog out of the tank and putting it on the table, he said, 'Jump!' The frog jumped.

Taking a scalpel, he amputated one of the frog's front legs. 'Jump!' he shouted. The frog jumped.

He amputated a hind leg. 'Jump!' The frog managed a respectable jump.

Amputating a third limb, the professor repeated his command. Bleeding profusely by now, the frog managed a feeble bounce.

Taking the scalpel to the fourth leg, the professor said, 'Jump'! No response from the frog. 'I said *jump*!' shouted the professor. The frog didn't move. 'JUMP!' he bellowed in the ear of the inert animal. No movement whatsoever, and finally the scientist gave up, considering the experiment at an end.

Taking his notebook from the shelf, the Irish scientist carefully noted, 'When all limbs are amputated, it is observed that the frog goes deaf.'

●

What has a hundred balls and fucks rabbits?

A shotgun.

●

What did the termite say when he walked into the nightclub?

'Is the bar tender here?'

●

Desperate because her husband hadn't made love to her in months, a lonely housewife finally mustered her courage and went to their doctor for advice. The doctor was very sympathetic and wrote out a prescription for pills that were guaranteed to rekindle the husband's ardour in a big way. 'They'll make him as horny as hell,' the doctor confided, 'but they're very potent, so just put *one* in whatever he's drinking.'

Upon driving home, the woman left the pills on the kitchen counter and dashed off to the supermarket. It didn't take long before the cat jumped up, knocked them over on to the floor, and ate a couple, as did the family dog. And when the husband got home with a headache, he took a few, thinking they were aspirin.

When the housewife returned, she was horrified to see the dog humping the cat and the cat jumping all over the dog, but even stranger was the sight of her husband with his penis inside the pencil sharpener. 'What in heaven's name are you doing, Fred?' she cried.

'See that mosquito?' he said.

●

What are the three reasons why sex is better with sheep?

They're always in the mood.
They never have a headache.
When you've finished screwing them, you can eat them.

●

The Smiths were very proud of their parrot, which was so intelligent that it could instantly repeat anything said to it. This was an especially big hit when they entertained, as the parrot would perch on the piano and announce the names of the arriving guests.

The only problem with the parrot was that he couldn't stay clear of the neighbour's prize chickens. The first time the neighbour caught him on top of the hens, he was returned with a stern warning; the next time he was confined to his perch for a week; but nothing worked. Caught in the act yet again, the parrot was punished by having all the feathers of his head shaved off.

The very next evening the Smiths were entertaining, and the parrot took his customary position on the piano. The first couple arrived, the hostess whispered to the bird, 'The Murphys,' and the bird spoke up, 'Announcing the Murphys.' All went according to schedule and the last guests were trickling in, when the door opened to admit the hostess's father-in-law, elderly and extremely bald. Before Mrs Smith had a chance to cue him, the bird trumpeted, 'Announcing the Chicken Fucker!'

●

What do you do when an elephant comes in your window?

Swim for your life.

●

How can you make your turtle fast?

Don't feed him.

●

This young woman was very fond of her pet parrot but finally could no longer put up with one of its very embarrassing habits. Whenever she would return to her apartment with a man, the bird would screech, 'Someone's going to get some tonight!' So she took it into the vet to see whether he could recommend any treatment.

The vet explained that it was simply a question of the bird being lonely and in need of female companionship, so the next stop was the pet shop. 'I'm afraid we're out of parrots at the moment,' said the proprietor, 'but in the meantime, why don't you take home this nice lady owl and see how they get along.'

A few nights later the young woman came back to the apartment with a handsome young acquaintance, but no sooner had the door opened than the parrot shrieked, 'Someone's going to get some tonight!'

'Whoooo?' hooted the owl.

The parrot glared at the owl. 'Not *you*, you big-eyed bitch!'

●

A newly recruited French Legionnaire found himself stationed in a remote fort in the desert. After a few weeks had gone by, he took one of the old-timers aside and asked what the men did for a good time. 'We use a camel' was the taciturn reply. Revolted, the young soldier turned his thoughts elsewhere, but as time went by and he got hornier and hornier, he could think of little else. Taking aside another veteran soldier, he asked the same question and got the same answer. 'We use the camel.' Finally, desperate, the young man accepted the fact that the camel was the only available outlet, and one night he sneaked out to the barn. As luck would have it, one of the old-timers wandered by the barn around the same time and caught sight of the young soldier up on a crate, screwing the camel. 'What the hell are you doing?' he called out.

Rather puzzled, the recruit said, 'I thought you said you used the camel for a good time.'

'Yes, but usually we just ride him into town.'

●

A journalist found himself sent to an even more remote desert encampment to do a story on the Spartan life of these tough desert fighters. Observing that there was no town, not even an oasis, for hundreds of miles, he couldn't resist asking the drill sergeant what the men did when their sexual urges get the better of them.

'We do have camels, you know,' was the answer.

'Gosh, that's an awful long ride to town,' commented the journalist.

'That's not exactly the plan,' said the sergeant. 'You'll see in a minute.' And pretty soon over a sand dune appeared a herd of frantic camels being furiously pursued by an entire battalion of soldiers with their pants around their knees. Unable to believe his eyes, the journalist gasped, 'No . . . It can't be. You mean they're in that much of a hurry just to screw a camel?'

To this the sergeant, unbuckling his khakis, replied, 'You wouldn't want to be left with an ugly one, would you?'

●

What do you get when you cross a skin doctor and an elephant?

A pachydermatologist.

●

Very concerned because his hens were laying fewer and fewer eggs each week, a farmer finally pinpointed the blame on his ageing rooster, who clearly wasn't fulfilling his henhouse responsibilities. So he went out and bought a young rooster. Eyeing the newcomer, the old rooster said, 'Listen, let's make a deal: I'll just take three hens, move over to that far corner, and leave all the rest to you.'

'Not a chance,' said the youngster. 'This is my henhouse now and all the females are mine.'

'Very well,' said the old rooster humbly, 'but perhaps you'd do me one small favour to save my pride. Let's have a race and the winner gets the henhouse; that way it won't look as though I'm being replaced because I can't perform any more.'

Sizing up his rickety competitor, the young cock agreed, even granting him a four-length handicap. Off they started around the course, but it soon became evident that the four-length lead wasn't going to hold for long. Pretty soon it was down to two lengths, and as they rounded the turn, going flat out, the youngster was just about to overtake the old rooster. Just then the farmer stepped out on to his porch, grabbed his shotgun, and blasted the new bird into smithereens. 'Dammit!' he said as he set the gun down, 'That's the third gay rooster I've bought this month.'

●

A retired schoolteacher finally realized she was tired of living alone and wanted some companionship, so after a good deal of thought she decided to visit the local pet shop. The owner suggested a parrot, with which she could conduct a civilized conversation. This seemed an excellent idea, so she bought a handsome parrot, sat him on a perch in her living room, and said, 'Say "Pretty boy". Silence from the bird. 'Come on, now, say "Pretty boy . . . pretty boy".'

At long last, disgustedly, the bird said, 'Oh, shit.'

Shocked, the schoolteacher said, 'Just for that, you get five minutes in the refrigerator.' Five minutes later she put the shivering bird back on its perch and said, 'Now let's hear it: "Pretty boy . . . pretty boy".'

'Lay off, for Christ's sake, would you!' said the parrot.

Outraged, the woman grabbed the bird and said, 'That's it! Ten minutes in the freezer,' and slammed the door on him.

Hopping about to keep warm, what does the parrot came across but a frozen turkey waiting for Christmas. Startled, he squawks, 'My God, *you* must have told the bitch to go fuck herself!'

●

This man goes to the hospital and is diagnosed as having a tapeworm. 'They're not easy to get rid of,' says the doctor, who tells the man to come in every day for two weeks, bringing a ginger biscuit and a hard-boiled egg. Grimacing, the patient agrees, and shows up on time the next morning. To his horror, the doctor shoves the egg up the man's asshole, then follows it with the crumbled-up biscuit. This goes on for twelve more days, after which the

39

doctor tells him to come in the next day with a hard-boiled egg and a hammer. On the last day the patient drops his pants, the doctor shoves in the egg, and waits. A few minutes later the worm pokes his head out, demands, 'Where the hell's my biscuit?' and *wham*—that's the end of the worm.

●

If you find H_2O inside a fire hydrant, what do you find outside?

K9P.

●

Why did the monkey fall out of the tree?
It was dead.

Why did the chicken fall out of the tree?
It was stapled to the monkey.

●

A little boy came into the house and said, 'Mummy, how much air does an Airedale need?
'I don't know,' she answered. 'Why?'
'Because I just saw one pumping up another one.'

●

What goes 'Hoppity . . . clank . . . hoppity . . . clank?'

The Easter Bunny with polio.

●

Once there was this city boy who wanted to go and live off the land, so he headed out to a farm to buy some animals. 'I'll take one of these,' he said to the farmer. 'What is it?'
'Well, to me it's a cock but to you it's a rooster,' said the farmer.
'I'll take one of these too,' said the city boy. 'What is it?'
'Well, to me it's a pullet but to you it's a chicken,' replied the farmer.

'Okay,' said the city boy. 'And I'll take one of those too, if you'll tell me what it is.'

'To me it's an ass but to you it's a mule,' explained the farmer, 'and when that ass gets stubborn, it sits down and you have to scratch its belly to get it moving again.'

So the city boy set off down the road with all of his new purchases. He was doing fine till a pretty girl drove by, at which point the ass sat down and refused to budge. Seeing he was having some trouble, the girl backed up and asked if there was anything she could do to help.

'Actually, yes,' said the city boy. 'Will you hold my cock and pullet while I scratch my ass?'

•

What did the grape do when the elephant sat on it?

It let out a little wine.

•

Why do mice have such small balls?

They can't dance.

•

Arab saying: *A woman for sons, a boy for pleasure, and a goat for sheer ecstasy.*

•

Australia: Where men are men and sheep are nervous.

•

What's grosser than gross?

One dog giving a blow-job to another dog.

•

A huge white horse walks into a bar, leans his hooves on the counter, and asks for a beer. Serving him, the barman can't resist commenting, 'You know, we've got a brand of whisky named after you.'

'What, Eric Whisky?' says the horse. 'Never heard of it.'

41

What's green and hangs from trees?

Giraffe snot.

A man suspects his wife of cheating on him so he goes to the pet shop to buy a parrot. He sees quite an assortment for sale from two hundred to a thousand pounds, but that's more than he wants to spend, so he's delighted to come across one in the corner for sale for £30. 'How come that one's so cheap?' he asks the sales assistant.

'To tell you the truth, his dick's oversized and embarrasses the customers,' is the explanation. The husband buys the bird anyway, and installs it on a perch right over the bed.

The next day the first thing he does after coming home from work is to rush upstairs. 'Well, what happened today?' he demands of the bird.

'Well, the milkman came, and . . . your wife told him to come into the bedroom, and . . . they took off their clothes, and . . . got into bed.'

'So what happened next,' screams the irate husband.

'I don't know,' says the parrot. 'I got a hard-on and fell off my perch.'

Why did the pervert cross the road?

Because his dick was stuck in the chicken.

One day this farmer was bragging to his neighbour that his dog was so smart he could count. Of course, the other farmer didn't believe him, so the first farmer ordered his dog to go down to the pond and count the ducks. The dog took off, came back, and barked four times, and when the farmers walked down to the pond, sure enough there were four ducks in sight.

Back at the farmhouse the neighbour confessed he was still sceptical, so the farmer sent the dog off again. This time the dog came back and barked six times, and sure enough there were six ducks on the pond.

When the neighbour was still unsatisfied, the farmer agreed to test the dog one more time and off the dog ran. On his return he started humping his master's leg, then picked up a stick and started shaking it.

'I knew that fool of a dog couldn't count,' said the neighbour triumphantly.

'Oh, yes he can,' said the farmer, 'you just can't understand him. He just said there are more fucking ducks than you can shake a stick at.'

●

What did the doe say as she rushed out of the woods?

'I'll never do that for two bucks again!'

●

What do you do with a bird with no wings?

Take it for a spin.

●

What do you call a person who can't walk through a pasture without getting shit all over their shoes?

An incowpoop.

●

One day a mouse was driving along the road in his Mercedes when he heard an anguished roaring noise coming from the side of the road. Stopping the car, he got out and discovered a lion stuck in a deep ditch and roaring for help. Reassuring the lion, the mouse tied a rope around the axle of the Mercedes, threw the other end down to the lion, and pulled the beast out of the ditch. The lion thanked the mouse profusely and they went their separate ways.

Two weeks later the lion was out for a stroll in the country when he heard a panicked squeaking coming from the side of the road. Investigating the noise, what should he come across but the mouse in the same hole. 'Oh, please help me, Mr Lion,' squeaked the terrified mouse. 'I saved you with my car once, remember?'

'Course I'll help you, little fellow,' roared the lion. 'I'll just lower my dick down to you, you hold on to it, and we'll have you out of there in a jiffy.' Sure enough, a few minutes later the mouse was high and dry on the roadside, trying to convey his eternal gratitude to the lion.

'Don't give it another thought,' said the lion kindly. 'It just goes to show that if you've got a big dick, you don't need a Mercedes.'

●

Male Anatomy

A man is strolling on the beach when he comes across a lamp lying in the sand. He rubs it and, sure enough, a genie pops out. 'I will grant you your one true desire,' booms the huge, turbaned figure.

'Wow, that's really great!' exclaims the man. 'I wish my dick touched the ground.'

So the genie cut his legs off.

•

Why is life like a penis?

Because when it's soft it's hard to beat, but when it's hard you get screwed.

•

Being a virgin, Bob was very nervous about his upcoming wedding night, so he decided to talk it over with his friend John, who was quite a man about town. 'Relax, Bob,' counselled John, 'you grew up on a farm: Just do like the dogs do.'

After the honeymoon the bride stormed over to her mother's house and announced that she's never going to live with Bob again. 'He's totally disgusting,' she wailed to her mother. Her mother asked what the problem was, and just what it was he did that was so disgusting. The bride blushed and refused to tell, but finally broke down. 'Ma, he doesn't know how to make love at all. . . . He just keeps smelling my ass and pissing on the bedpost!'

●

Why do Texan girls walk bowlegged?

Everything's big in Texas!

●

A salesman who is on the road is staying in a futuristic motel. He has an important sales call the next morning, and realizing he needs a trim, he calls the desk clerk to inquire whether there is a barber on the premises. 'I'm afraid not, sir,' said the clerk, 'but down the hall there's a bank of vending machines and one will give you a haircut.' Thoroughly intrigued, the salesman finds the machine, inserts fifty pence, and sticks his head in the opening. The machine starts buzzing and whirring. Fifteen seconds later he pulls out his head and discovers he's got the best haircut he's ever had.

Two feet away is another machine that says MANICURES 50p, and the salesman thinks, Why not? So he pays the money, inserts his hands into the slot, and out they come with a terrific manicure.

The next machine has a big sign: THIS MACHINE DOES WHAT MEN NEED MOST WHEN AWAY FROM THEIR WIVES. The salesman looks both ways, unzips his fly, inserts his dick, and puts in the fifty pence. The machine buzzes away as the guy screams in excruciating pain. Fifteen seconds later it stops and he pulls his dick out with trembling hands: There's a button sewed to the tip.

●

A man went into the corner chemist and confided that two lovely young stewardesses were coming to spend the whole weekend at his flat. 'I need something to get it hard and keep it hard for the whole two days.' The pharmacist insisted that he couldn't dispense any such drug without a prescription, but after a long and detailed inventory of the stewardesses' charms, he relented and gave the man a little bottle. 'Use it sparingly,' the pharmacist cautioned. 'It's very strong stuff.'

When he opened the shop on Monday morning, the pharmacist was horrified to see the man crawling towards him on the pavement, bloody and battered, his clothes in tatters. As he reached the door, he whispered, 'Please, you've gotta get me some Deep Heat.'

'Christ, man,' said the pharmacist, 'you can't put Deep Heat on your cock. You'll die from the pain!'

The guy gasped, 'It's not for my cock, it's for my elbow: The stewardesses never showed up!'

●

Two New York winos, Rick and Billy, woke up in an alley in dire need of a drink but with only sixty cents between them. 'Shay, I got an idea,' said Rick. He used the money to purchase a hot dog from the nearest vendor, then pulled Billy after him into the nearest bar and ordered a round of drinks. After downing them, seeing the barman heading their way with the bill, Rick quickly inserted the hot dog in Billy's fly and began to suck on the end of it. 'Get the hell out of here, you goddamn fags.' This worked equally well at the next bar, and the next, and the next - in fact, all through the day - when they finally crawled back to their spot in the alley, dead drunk. 'Ya shee what you can do with a hot dog?' slurred Rick cheerfully.

'What hot dog?' laughed Billy. 'We losht the hot dog after the third bar.'

●

Why do boys run faster than girls?

They have two ball bearings and a stick shift.

●

A man steps into this little backwoods restaurant for lunch, and after finishing his meal he inquires the way to the men's room. Told that it's around the back of the building he heads through the back door, finds the outhouse, and takes a shit, only to discover there's no toilet paper. But there is a sign on the wall that reads, WIPE YOURSELF WITH YOUR FINGER, THEN INSERT FINGER INTO THIS HOLE, AND YOUR FINGER WILL BE CLEANED WITH GREAT ATTENTION. So the man wipes up and sticks his finger through the hole.

On the other side is standing a little boy holding a brick in either hand, who claps them together at the sight of the finger poking through. The guy screams in pain, yanks his hand back, and starts sucking his finger.

●

This fellow had been assured by his fiancée that she was a virgin, but given the state of modern morals, he didn't completely trust her. So on their wedding night he had a little trick question ready for her. Pulling down his pyjamas and revealing his dick, he asked, 'Now dear, do you know what this is?'

'That's a wee-wee,' she answered coyly.

Very pleased with her naiveté, he said gently, 'No, sweety, it's a penis.'

'Uh-uh, it's a wee-wee,' she insisted, shaking her head.

A little annoyed, he said, 'You've got to learn a few things, dear. Now, this is a penis.'

'It can't be,' she retorted. 'It's not half as big as some of the penises I've seen.'

●

Mr Jones went to the sex therapist as a last resort, confiding in him that his sex life at home was terrible. The doctor leaned back in his big leather chair and said, 'I advise having a few martinis first to loosen things up; then let your mind roam over how exciting the whole business of sex used to be.' They glanced out the window, where two dogs happened to be banging away with great abandon in the garden. 'Now, look at the excitement and vitality of those animals,' said the doctor. 'Go home, have a few martinis, and think about the spontaneity of those

48

dogs out in the garden. Then come back and see me in two weeks.'

Two weeks later the doctor asked, 'Well, how'd it go?'

'Terrible,' said the patient. 'It took seven martinis just to get her out in the garden.'

●

What did the doctor say to the nervous patient in the waiting room about his upcoming circumcision?

'It won't be long now.'

●

A well-dressed man walked into a nice bar in the small town. Ordering two martinis, he drank one down, then poured the second on his hand. Unable to contain his curiosity, the barman leaned over and said, 'I hope you don't mind me asking, sir, but why did you waste a good drink?'

The man replied, 'I just want to get my date drunk.'

●

During his monthly visit to the corner barbershop, this man asked his barber if he had any advice about how to treat his growing baldness. After a small silence the barber leaned over and confided that the best thing he'd come across was, er, female juices.

'But you're balder than I am!' protested the customer.

'True,' said the barber, 'but you've got to admit, I've got one hell of a moustache.'

●

An extremely obese man shows up at his doctor's surgery and claims that he's tried every possible way to lose weight, to no avail. So the doctor proposes a radical diet: rectal feeding. Reassuring the fattie that he won't starve to death, the doctor explains that he can actually take in enough nutrients through the rectal walls to sustain life, but that he's sure to lose weight in the process.

Three weeks later the patient comes in for a follow-up appointment, and he's down from 360 to a trim 175 pounds. The doctor, shows him into his surgery and asks him how's he's feeling, noticing that he's bouncing up and down in his seat quite energetically. 'I'm feeling great, doctor; never felt better,' is the reply.

'In that case, why are you bouncing up and down like that?' asked the doctor.

'Just chewing some gum!'

•

Three men stopped at a big house in the country to ask for a room for the night. When their hostess showed them to their rooms, she had one request: that they not look inside a big cupboard on the landing. The men resisted the temptation all night, but in the morning they opened the doors. Their hostess found them staring at a collection of hundreds of penises nailed to the doors and walls of the cupboard. 'Well men, you asked for it,' she said, then asked the first one, 'What does your dad do?'

'My dad's a butcher,' he stammered.

The woman took a meat cleaver and chopped off the first man's dick and nailed it to the wall. 'And what does your father do?' she asked the second man.

'My father's a carpenter,' he quavered.

So the hostess took a jigsaw, cut off his cock, and nailed it to the wall. 'And your dad?' she asked the third man.

'Well, my dad's a lollipop manufacturer: You're going to have to suck mine off.'

•

Once upon a time, King Arthur was preparing for a long campaign. Wanting to make sure the lovely Guinevere was safe from temptation, the king had her fitted with an ingenious chastity belt designed to amputate anything attempting penetration. Returning victorious from the battlefield six months later, the suspicious ruler ordered all the palace retainers to strip off their pants in the courtyard. One by one, Arthur saw stumps where their penises had been, except for one fellow at the end of the line. 'One amongst you at least is a man strong enough to resist temptation: a man of honour,' he cried. 'What is your name?'

'Aaaghkuggh.'

●

What's the problem with oral sex?

The view.

●

One morning a milkman called on one of his regular customers and was surprised to see a white bed sheet with a hole in the middle hanging up in her living room. The housewife explained that she'd had a party the night before. They had played a game called 'Who's Who' in which each of the men had put their equipment through the hole and the women tried to guess their identity.

'Gosh, that sounds fun,' said the milkman. 'I wish I'd been here.'

'You should have been,' said the housewife. 'Your name came up three times.'

●

A man with a two-inch prick walks into a whorehouse and drops his pants in front of one of the girls, who says, 'Just who do you think you're going to please with that little thing?'

And the man says, 'Me.'

●

What did the flasher say to the woman in sub-zero weather?

'It's so cold – could I just describe myself?'

●

51

The newlyweds were undressing in their honeymoon suite on the wedding night. The new husband, who was a big bruiser of a guy, tossed his pants over to his wife and said, 'Here, put these on.'

Puzzled, she pulled them on and said, 'These would fit two of me - I can't wear these pants.'

'That's right,' said the husband, 'and don't you forget it. I'm the one who wears the trousers in this family.'

With that the wife threw her pants over to his side of the bed and said, 'Try these on.'

Finding he could only get them up as far as his knees, her husband said, 'Hell, I can't even get *into* your pants.'

'That's right,' she snapped, 'and that's the way it's going to be until your damn attitude changes.'

•

What makes a man think he's so great?
 - He has a bellybutton that won't work.
 - He has tits that won't give milk.
 - He has a cock that won't crow.
 - He has balls that won't roll.
 - He has an ass that won't carry a thing.

Hey, what are you smiling for? Your pussy won't catch mice.

•

Little Billy asked his father, 'Dad, what's a penis?'

Without missing a beat, his father unzipped his fly, pulled it out, and said, 'Son, *this* is a penis. And, I might add, it's a perfect penis.'

'Thanks, Dad,' said little Billy, and ran over to his best friend's house to tell him about this new revelation.

'Really?' said his friend in amazement. 'Well what did he show you?'

'This,' said the little boy, unzipping his own pants and taking out his prick. 'And you know what? If it was just a little bit shorter, it'd be just as perfect as my dad's.'

Why did God make man first?

He didn't want a woman looking over his shoulder.

●

A married woman is entertaining her lover one rainy afternoon when her husband unexpectedly comes home early from work. 'Quick, out on the roof,' hisses the woman, pushing him out the bedroom window and closing it just as her husband's footsteps reach the top of the stairs.

Crouched on the roof in the rain, the boyfriend is naked except for a rubber and is wondering what the hell his next move should be. The first person in sight is a jogger, and the boyfriend takes a deep breath, jumps off the roof, and falls into step alongside the jogger as nonchalantly as possible. After a block and a half the jogger can no longer contain his curiosity and asks, 'Hey, do you always wear that thing when you run?'

'Nah,' says the boyfriend coolly, 'only when it rains.'

●

A recent poll uncovered the fact that 90 per cent of all men masturbate in the shower. The other 10 per cent sing. Do you know what they sing?

- You say you don't know! I didn't think so. . . .

●

A travelling salesman was looking for a place to spend the night and a local farmer offered to take him in if he didn't mind sharing quarters with his daughter. The salesman said that would be fine.

A few months later the salesman received the following letter from the farmer:

Are you the guy who did the pushin'?

Left the grease spots on the cushion?

Left the footprints on the dashboard upside-down?

Ever since you left my Nellie
She's been swellin' round the belly
So you'd better come back to this here town.

The salesman replied by return post:
   Yes I'm the guy who did the pushin'
   Left the grease spots on the cushion
   Left the footprints on the dashboard upside-down.
   Ever since I left your Venus
   I've been itching round the penis,
   So I think we're pretty even all around.

●

What's long and red and hard and comes with balls?

A baseball bat.

●

A little girl walked into the bathroom, saw her father in the shower, and ran to her mother screaming, 'Mommy, Mommy! Daddy has a big ugly worm hanging out of his weewee!'

'That isn't a worm, sweetheart,' said her mother reassuringly. 'That's part of your daddy's body and a very important part. If your daddy didn't have one of those, you wouldn't be here. And come to think of it . . . neither would I.'

●

Having been at sea for three months, the sailor was extremely horny when they reached port. Heading straight for the nearest whorehouse, he asked the price.

'Seventy-five pounds,' replied the madam. It seemed a pretty steep price to the sailor, but he paid up and was shown to a room to await the girl. When the whore opened the door, she saw the sailor masturbating furiously on the bed. 'Stop, stop,' she cried. 'What're you doing?'

'Hey, for seventy-five pounds you don't think I'm going to let you have the easy one, do you?'

One day Little Herbie heard a noise from his parents' room and opened the door to see them screwing. 'What're you doing, Dad?' he asked.

'Just playing gin rummy with your mother,' was the answer.

On the way back downstairs Little Herbie heard a noise coming from his grandparents' room, opened the door, and asked what was going on. His grandad explained he was just playing gin rummy with his grandmother.

Not too much later, dinner was served and everyone came to the table except Little Herbie. Looking in his room, Herbie's father found him lying on his bed, the sheets flapping up and down. 'I'm just playing gin rummy,' explained the boy.

'But you've got no one to play with,' said his dad sternly.

'That's OK, Dad; with a hand like this, you don't need a partner.'

●

A farmer needed help as he realized his manhood was failing him, so he asked his doctor for a cure. The doctor gave him a small container of pills and told him to take no more than one a week. Back at the farm, the farmer thought he'd try the medication out on his stud horse first. The horse swallowed the pill, jumped out of his stall, kicked a side of the barn down, and ran off down the road. Those pills are too strong for me, the farmer thought, and he poured the rest into the well.

Later, when the doctor asked the farmer how the pills were working, the farmer said he had thrown them down the well. 'Heavens!' the doctor exclaimed. 'You haven't drunk any of the water, have you?'

'No,' the farmer said, 'we can't get the pump handle down.'

●

One day when the teacher walked to the blackboard, she noticed someone had written the word 'PENIS' in tiny letters. She turned around and scanned the class looking for a guilty face. Finding none, she quickly erased it and began class.

The next day she went into the room she noticed in larger letters, written about halfway across the board the word 'PENIS'. Again, she looked around in vain for the culprit, so she proceeded with the day's lesson.

Every morning for about a week, she went into the classroom and found the word 'PENIS' written on the board, each day's letters larger than the previous one's. Finally, one day, she walked in expecting to find the word 'PENIS' on the board and instead found the words: 'The more you rub it, the bigger it gets.'

●

A carpenter, an electrician and a dentist had a mutual friend who was getting married, and, in keeping with the custom, each was determined to play a practical joke on the newlyweds. The electrician decided to wire up the marriage bed so that when the two bodies touched, they got a shock. The carpenter planned to saw partly through the bed-frame so that it would collapse when the shocked newlyweds jumped apart. And as the wedding approached, the dentist was still scratching his head and trying to come up with something.

After the honeymoon the new husband confronted his three friends. 'I didn't mind too much when we got electric-shocked,' he told them, 'and we both got a good laugh when the bed fell down. But who the hell put Novocaine in the Vaseline?'

●

A Scotsman stopped off for a few drinks at his local pub. On his way home he was having trouble navigating, so he decided to take a little rest by the roadside. As he was snoring gently, two girls came by and one said to the other, 'You know, they say Scotsmen go naked under their kilts – shall we see if it's true?'

Her companion eagerly agreed, and when they lifted his kilt they found the story to be indeed true. In fact, what greeted their eyes was so pleasing that one of the girls took her blue hair-ribbon and tied it around the man's dick as he slept.

Not too much later the Scotsman awoke, and when he stood up to take a pee he got quite a start at the sight of the blue ribbon. 'Hoots man!' he exclaimed. 'I don't know what you've been up to, but I'm certainly glad to see you took first place.'

●

Why is it only women get haemorrhoids?

Because when God created man, He created the perfect asshole.

●

One day Bobby's teacher tells the class they're going to play a thinking game, and asks for a volunteer. 'Pick me, pick me,' begs Bobby.

'Okay, Bobby,' says the teacher. 'Now I'm going to describe objects to you, and you tell me what they are. Here we go: what's red, shiny, and you eat it?'

'A cherry,' says Bobby.

'No, it's an apple, but it shows you're thinking,' said the teacher gently. 'Ready for the next one? What's yellow and you eat it?'

'A lemon,' says Bobby.

'No,' says the teacher, 'it's a banana, but it shows you're thinking.'

Before the teacher can continue, Bobby interrupts. 'Okay, teacher, I've got one for you.' He reaches into his pocket, looks down, pulls his hand out, and asks, 'What's long, pink, and has a little red head on the end of it?'

'Oooh, Bobby!' squeals the teacher.

'No, it's a match – but it shows you're thinking.'

●

One day this man woke up to find that he had three bright red circles around the base of his penis. Panicked, he rushed to the doctor, thinking he'd contracted some new kind of herpes or VD. The doctor was equally puzzled by the symptoms, gave the man a course of antibiotics, and told him to come back in a week if the rings didn't clear up.

A week later the fellow was back in the doctor's surgery, but the second dose of medication had no effect either. On his third visit, the doctor told the man to try various creams, soaps and lotions. The next day the patient was back. 'It worked, it worked!' he announced ecstatically.

'Oh really? And what did you use to get rid of the rings?' asked the doctor.

'Lipstick remover.'

●

Three friends were out enjoying a night on the town, and the suggestion that they visit the local whorehouse met with enthusiasm all around – especially when the madam told them there was a special offer that evening. For £50, £75 or £100, the customer would receive a sexual treat beyond his wildest dreams.

The first man forks out £50, is shown to the first door on the right, and soon his friends hear cries of ecstasy coming from within. He emerges some time later, still sweaty and out of breath and grinning from ear to ear. 'She's the most beautiful woman I've ever seen,' he says happily, and goes on to explain that after extensive foreplay she had put two pineapple rings around his penis and eaten them.

The second man can hardly wait to fork over his £75, is shown to a room, and soon wild cries of bliss can be heard. Eventually he returns with the same grin and the same story, except that he'd had whipped cream along with the two pineapple rings.

The third man needs little persuading to part with his £100 and is shown to an upstairs room. Soon cries of ecstasy can be heard, but his friends are puzzled when they're interrupted by a scream of agony. When he eventually returns, they can't wait to hear what happened. Yes, he explained wearily, she was the most beautiful woman he'd ever seen, and after extensive foreplay she had covered his prick with two pineapple rings, whipped cream, chopped nuts, and topped it off with a maraschino cherry.

'So then what happened?' asked his friends eagerly.

'Well,' he replied, 'it looked so good I ate it myself.'

●

What's green and is used to fry pricks?

A Peter Pan.

●

There was this guy who desperately wanted to have sex with his girlfriend. However, he was too embarrassed because of his extremely small penis. So one night, he took her to a dark place where she couldn't see it and, after furiously making out with her, dropped his trousers and put his penis in her hand.

'Sorry, I don't smoke,' she whispered.

●

Female Anatomy

How many men does it take to mop a floor?

None. It's a woman's job.

●

These two men coming home from work meet on the commuter train and begin chatting. They move on from sports and the weather to the subject of their wives. Says Fred, 'You should know that my wife is actually pretty ugly.'

'She may not be a beauty,' concedes Phil, 'but my wife is probably the ugliest woman on the face of the earth.'

They argue back and forth about whose wife is uglier until Fred resolves the dispute. 'You come over to my house, Phil, and meet my wife. If you still think your wife is uglier, we'll go over to your house to check her out.' So they go to the first man's house, have a drink with his wife, and then step outside. 'Well?' asks Fred.

'I've got to admit that your wife is ugly, but mine has her beaten cold,' says Phil. So they go to Phil's house. Fred is highly sceptical. Upon entering through the back door, Phil bends over, slides open a trapdoor, and yells, 'Sweety, come on up.'

She shouts back, 'Do you want me to put the bag over my head?'

'No,' he shouts back down, 'I don't want to screw you, I just want to show you to somebody.'

●

A guy and a girl are going at it hot and heavy in the backseat of his car. 'Put a finger inside me,' she moans. 'Now two . . . Now three . . .' and so on until his whole hand is inside her. Pretty soon, following her passionate instructions, both hands are inside, and she whispers, 'Put your head in.' He obliges and barely hears, 'Crawl in.'

So he's walking around in there, when he's startled by a voice in the darkness saying 'Who's there?' Another guy comes up out of the shadows and says, 'What are *you* doing in here?'

'Just looking around,' says the second man.

'Well, if you find some keys, hand 'em over and we can drive my truck out of here.'

●

A woman walks into a bar with a duck under her arm. One of the drunks at the bar turns and says, 'That has got to be the ugliest pig I've ever seen.'

The woman says, 'That's not a pig, it's a duck.'

The drunk answers, 'I was talking to the duck.'

●

Heard about the nutty geneticist in southern California?

He's trying to cross a Mexican jumping bean with a cucumber in order to create the world's first organic vibrator.

●

What's the purpose of a belly button?

It's a place to put your gum in on the way down.

●

Some friends decide to help out a buddy who is still a virgin and very naive about sex. They hire an obliging prostitute for their friend for the afternoon, unaware that she had chilli for lunch. Because the guy is so naive, she suggests some '69' to start. While they're going down on each other, she can't hold in a giant, pungent fart. A few minutes later she lets out another one, right in his face.

The fellow jumps up and says, 'This really feels good, but I don't think I can take sixty-seven more of those farts.'

●

One day a certain housewife was going about the usual business of cleaning the house when she suddenly felt intensely horny. Unfortunately her husband was still at work, so she resorted to stripping off all her clothes and starting to masturbate. She got pretty excited, rubbing herself and moaning, and when her husband walked in she was writhing in the middle of the living-room floor. He looked through the mail and said to his wife, 'Darling, when you've finished vacuuming the floor, could you get started on dinner?'

●

Why are most cowgirls bowlegged?

Because cowboys never take their hats off when they eat.

●

Did you hear about the prostitute who had an appendectomy?

The doctor sewed up the wrong hole, so now she's making money on the side.

●

What did the vampire say to the teacher?

'See you next period.'

●

The horny husband always seems to have a hard time convincing his wife to have sex. One night, just before climbing into bed, he hands her a glass of water and two aspirins.

'But I don't have a headache,' she protested.

'Gotcha!'

•

Why don't girls wear dresses in the winter?

Chapped lips.

•

These three men went for a drive in the country and their car broke down, so they went to the nearest farmhouse to ask for shelter for the night. 'Sure, lads,' said the farmer, 'you can spend the night here, but you've each got to sleep with one of my daughters, because they don't get much company out here.' The men all agreed, and during the night the farmer got up to make sure they were going through with their part of the deal.

The next morning the men went on their way and the farmer called his daughters together. 'Linda, why were you laughing last night?'

'Because it tickled, Daddy.'

'Susie, why were you crying?'

'Because it hurt, Daddy.'

'Lizzie, why was your room silent?'

'Because you always told me not to talk with my mouth full.'

•

A man said to a hooker, 'What would your mother say if she saw you doing this?'

'She'd kill me. I'm on her corner.'

•

Rule at the girls' school: lights out at ten, candles out at ten-thirty.

•

A college professor had a reputation for offending women in his anthropology classes, so a bunch of students got together and agreed to walk out the next time it happened. The next week, while discussing an obscure African tribe, the professor leered and said, 'The men over there have penises twelve inches long!'

The students rose and headed for the door.

'Oh, come on, girls,' snickered the professor, 'the plane doesn't leave till Sunday.'

●

What's the ultimate in punk?

A pubic Mohawk.

●

How do you make a hormone?

Put sawdust in the Vaseline.

●

How can you tell when a girl is horny?

When you put your hand down her pants and it feels like a horse eating oats.

●

What do you call the area between the vagina and the asshole?

A chin rest.

●

What are three things a woman can do that a man can't?

(1) Have a baby.
(2) Have her period.
(3) Get laid when she's dead.

●

Did you hear about the two sailors and the nurse who were stranded together on a desert island?

After three months the nurse was so disgusted with what she was doing that she killed herself.

After three more months the sailors were so disgusted with what they were doing that they buried her.

●

What's the difference between a young whore and an old whore?

A young whore uses Vaseline and an old whore uses Poli-Grip.

●

Hungry after overseeing the delivery of his cattle to a Chicago stockyard, a cowboy headed to a nearby restaurant for dinner. The only vacant seat was next to a young, wealthy, and well-educated young lady, and the cowboy couldn't help overhearing her place her order: 'I'll have breast of fowl - virgin fowl. Make sure it's a virgin: Catch it yourself. Garnish my plate with onions and bring me a cup of coffee, not too hot and not too cold. Oh, and, waiter, open the window: I smell horse; there must be a cowboy in the house.'

Thoroughly pissed off, the cowboy proceeded to place his own order: 'I'll have duck - fucked duck: Fuck it yourself. Garnish my plate with horseshit, then bring me a cup of coffee as strong as Texas mule piss, and blow the foam off with a fart. Oh, and, waiter, knock down the wall. I smell cunt: there must be a whore in the house.'

●

What's the ultimate embarrassment for a woman?

Taking her German shepherd to the vet and finding out he has the clap.

●

How many animals can you find in a pair of pantyhose?

Two calves; ten little piggies; one ass; one pussy; one thousand hares; maybe some crabs; and a dead fish nobody can find.

●

A mother and daughter lived together in devastating poverty, so it was cause for great rejoicing when, on her way home from school, the daughter found fifty pence on the sidewalk. She ran home and showed it to her mother, who decided that for fifty pence they could get two eggs and a bottle of ketchup and have a real meal. So off went the daughter to the store.

As luck would have it, the daughter was happily skipping home with the eggs and ketchup when a truck backfired, startling her so much that she dropped the groceries. Staring down at the ruined feast, which was smashed at her feet, she sat down and started to cry.

A man came up behind her and surveyed the scene for a few moments. 'There there, honey, don't cry,' he said consolingly. 'It would have died anyway: It's eyes were too far apart.'

●

Why is a clitoris like Antarctica?

Most men know it's there, but few really care.

●

What's the best thing about Women's Liberation?

It gives you girls something to do in your spare time!

●

A young lady walks into a chemist's and asks the pharmacist for a gross of condoms. Thinking that an order of that magnitude deserves a snappy answer, the pharmacist asks what size she would like.

'Oh, mix them up,' she replies. 'I'm not going steady.'

•

An employee of a factory that makes all sorts of rubber goods, from tyres to rubber bands, was giving some guests a factory tour. Of special interest was the condom plant, where rubbers were being peeled off cock-shaped moulds and rolled up for packaging. But every twelfth one was shuttled aside and a small hole was punched in it. Shocked, one of the visitors exclaimed, 'What are you doing? Think of all the unwanted pregnancies that's going to cause!'

'Yes,' said the employee, 'but it certainly helps sales for our nipple division.'

•

Sadly neglected by her husband, a horny housewife turned to her next-door neighbour for advice. 'Why don't you order your milk from the milkman,' was the suggestion, 'and when the bill comes, see if you can settle it with sex.' This seemed like an excellent idea, and sure enough, when the bill was presented, the milkman was delighted to settle for a long and energetic screw. Putting his trousers back on, the milkman reached for the bill to mark it 'Paid in Full'.

'Oh, no you don't,' said the housewife, grabbing the bill. 'You brought me this milk a quart at a time, and that's the way I'm going to pay for it.'

•

After going through pre-natal classes with his expectant wife, the proud new father remained by his wife's bedside throughout labour and birth, bonding with the newborn child. Wanting to be as sympathetic as possible, he took his wife's hand and said emotionally, 'Tell me how it was, darling, tell me how it actually felt to give birth.'

His wife replied, 'OK. Smile as hard as you can.'

Beaming down beautifully at his wife and child, the father said, 'That's not too hard.'

She continued, 'Now insert your index fingers into the corners of your mouth.' He obeyed, still smiling broadly.

'Now stretch your lips as far as they will go. . . .'

'Still not too tough,' he commented.

'Right,' she retorted. 'Now pull them over your head.'

•

Heard about the virginity restoration kit?

A needle, a thread, and a maraschino cherry.

•

As the newlywed couple were checking into the hotel for their honeymoon, another couple at the desk offered to show them around the town that night. Thanking them for the kind offer, the bridegroom explained that it was their wedding night and that they'd prefer to postpone the tour.

When the second couple came down to breakfast the next morning they were astonished to catch sight of the groom in the hotel bar apparently drowning his sorrows. 'Why, you should be the happiest man in the world today,' they said, coming over to him.

'Yesterday I was,' said the man mournfully, 'but this morning, without realizing it, I put three ten-pound notes on the pillow and got up to get dressed.'

'Hey, cheer up, she probably didn't even notice.'

'That's the problem,' the groom went on. 'Without even thinking, she gave me five pounds change.'

•

What's the difference between worry and panic?

About twenty-eight days.

•

A certain virginal and shy college freshman was lucky to have a room-mate who was considerably more experienced. When the bashful boy broke down and explained his predicament, his room-mate was quick to offer to set him up with the campus floozie. 'Just take her out to dinner and a show, and then let nature take its course,' he explained reassuringly. 'This girl knows what the score is.'

The room-mate arranged the date as promised, and the freshman took the girl student out for a delightful evening of dining and dancing. On the way home he parked his car in a dark lane, broke out in a cold sweat, and blurted out, 'Gosh, I sure would love to have a little pussy.'

'I would too,' she sighed. 'Mine's the size of a milk-pail.'

●

During intercourse a husband has a heart attack and dies. The next day the mortician informs the wife that the corpse still has a hard-on and he thinks it may look odd in the coffin. 'Fine,' says the wife. 'Cut it off and stick it up his ass.' Making absolutely sure he's heard correctly, the mortician obliges her wishes.

During the funeral a number of the deceased's friends and relations are perturbed to see a tear in the corner of his eye, but the widow assures them that there's no cause for concern. Just before the casket is closed, she leans over and quietly whispers in her dead husband's ear, 'It *hurts*, doesn't it?'

●

Fred came home from work in time to catch his wife sliding naked down the bannister. 'What the hell are you doing?' he demanded.

'Just heating up dinner, darling,' she cried.

●

A man and his wife were fooling around when she asked, 'Darling, could you take your ring off? It's hurting me.'

Her husband replies, 'Ring? Hell, that's my wristwatch.'

●

This woman goes to the gynaecologist for the first time and is rather embarrassed as she puts her feet in the stirrups. The doctor goes around for a look and says, 'Why, that's the biggest pussy I've ever seen – the biggest pussy I've ever seen!'

'You didn't have to say it twice,' snaps the woman.

'I didn't,' says the doctor.

●

What's the worst thing about having a cold when you've got your period?

Having your tampon pop out when you sneeze.

●

Why do women have longer fingernails?

Deeper penetration.

●

Know how to make a pussy talk?

Put a tongue in it.

●

A nymphomaniac goes to the supermarket and gets all hot and bothered eyeing the carrots and cucumbers. By the time she gets to the checkout line she can't hold out much longer, so she asks one of the supermarket baggers to carry her groceries out to the car for her. They're halfway across the lot when the nympho slips her hand down his pants and whispers, 'You know, I've got an itchy pussy.'

'Sorry, lady,' says the bagger, 'but I can't tell one of those Japanese cars from another.'

●

Two whores are walking down the street.

One remarks, 'I smell cock!'

The other replies, 'That's just my breath.'

A wife arriving home from a shopping trip was horrified to find her husband in bed with a lovely young thing. Just as she was about to storm out of the house, her husband stopped her with these words: 'Before you leave, I want you to hear how this all came about. While I was driving along the highway, I saw this young girl here, looking tired and bedraggled, so I brought her home and made her a meal from the roast beef you had forgotten in the refrigerator. She had only some worn-out sandals on her feet, so I gave her a pair of good shoes you had discarded because they had gone out of style. She was cold so I gave her a sweater I bought you for your birthday which you never wore because the colours didn't suit you. Her slacks were worn out, so I gave her a pair of yours that were perfectly good but too small for you now. Then, as she was about to leave the house, she paused and asked, "Is there anything else your wife doesn't use any more?"'

What do you give a hooker on her birthday?

A layer cake.

What's the difference between a woman and a volcano?

Volcanos don't fake eruptions.

Homosexuals

Why does it take two gay men to rape a girl?

One holds her down while the other does her hair.

●

What do you call a vampire in drag?

A transvestbite.

●

What's the definition of dried fruit?

A homosexual with a vasectomy.

●

What do lesbians do for dinner?

Eat out.

●

A crowd gathered around the wreck of a truck carrying designer gowns and accessories. Then from the back of the crowd came a hysterical voice, 'Please, please let me through: I'm a transvestite.'

●

Why do airlines pilots really like landing in San Francisco?

All they have to do is get the plane near the airport and they get sucked in.

How many straight San Francisco waiters does it take to change a light bulb?

Both of them.

●

A hot and dusty cowboy came into a bar, pounding his fist to get the bartender's attention, and said, 'I'm so thirsty I could lick the sweat off a cow's balls!'

A fag sitting in the corner overheard and piped up with 'Moo, moooo.'

●

What happens if you get on a bus full of queers?

You get off.

●

What's green, gay, and flies through the air?

Peter Pansy!

●

What did the constipated gay say to his boyfriend?

'With friends like you, who needs enemas?'

●

What do faggots do every twenty-eight days?

Stick a tampon up their assholes.

●

What do you get when you have 100 sex-crazed gays in the same room?

About a quart.

●

In a recent survey on why some men are homosexual, 82 per cent of the men surveyed responded that either genetics or home environment was the principal factor. The remaining 18 per cent revealed that they had been sucked into it.

●

What do you call a gay Smurf?

A Smaggot.

●

A gay man paid a visit to his doctor and confided that he had a vibrator stuck up his ass. 'Let me have a look,' said the doctor reassuringly. 'I'll have it out in no time.'

'Oh, doctor, please don't do that,' said the gay.

'What the hell do you want me to do?' asked the doctor.

'Change the batteries, please.'

●

Farmer Jones died during the winter, and when it came time for spring planting, Widow Jones realized she couldn't do all the work herself. So she applied to the town council, only to be told that all the able-bodied farmhands had already been hired and the only two left were an ex-con and a queer. Widow Jones chose the queer, and was pleased to find him a steady and reliable worker. When six weeks of hard labour had gone by, the man asked Widow Jones if he could have Saturday night off to go into town.

'All right,' she consented, 'but be back by nine o'clock.'

The farmhand wasn't back until ten-thirty, and as he tiptoed up the stairs he heard Widow Jones summon him to her room.

'Take off my shoes,' she commanded. He obeyed. 'Take off my dress.' He did so. 'Take off my slip . . . and my stockings . . . and my garter belt.'

The queer obeyed without saying a word.

'Now take off my bra,' snapped Widow Jones, 'and don't you ever borrow my clothes again!'

Three white men and two black men are hanging out at the corner bar and got into an argument over whose dick is bigger. Finally they realize there's only one way to resolve the dispute, so they walk over to a table and lay them all out. Just then a fag walks in, takes one look, and squeals, 'Ooooh, a buffet.'

●

What are cowboys who ride sidesaddle?

Gay caballeros.

●

What's a fag's favourite expression?

'Get a hold of yourself!'

●

Why was the American fag disappointed in his long-awaited trip to London?

He found out Big Ben was a clock.

●

What's the definition of a bisexual?

Someone who likes girls as well as the next guy.

●

'In the centre ring,' cries the ringmaster, 'we have Nero, the boldest and bravest animal-trainer in the world. Watch, ladies and gentlemen, as he puts his head between the jaws of our man-eating lion!' The crowd roars as Nero pulls out his head unscathed.

'Now, folks, watch this!' shouts the announcer, as Nero unzips his pants and puts his prick between the giant teeth. 'Don't do it!' shrieks the audience as the lion's jaws clamp shut. But without flinching Nero pulls them open and removes his unharmed penis, and wild cheers fill the arena.

When the noise dies down, the ringmaster steps forward and announces, 'Ladies and gentlemen, a prize of five thousand, yes five thousand pounds, to the man in our audience who'll try that trick.' His jaw drops as a small, effeminate man steps right up to the ringside. 'You're going to repeat that trick in front of all these people?' he asks incredulously.

'Certainly,' says the fag, 'but I must tell you something first. I don't think I can open my mouth as wide as the lion did.'

●

Did you hear about Calvin Klein's jeans for fags?

They have knee-pads in the front and a zipper at the back.

●

One Sunday in church, a homosexual decided to make a ten-pound contribution as the collection plate went by. Seeing his generosity, the preacher said, 'Brother, we'll let you pick out the next three hymns.'

The homosexual stood up and said, 'Oh, goody! I'll take him . . . and him . . . and him.'

●

'My dildo can do anything a man can do,' boasted a dyke in a bar one night.

'Oh yeah?' replied a nearby drunk, 'Let's see your dildo get up and order a round of drinks.'

●

What's the difference between a haematologist and a urologist?

A haemotologist pricks your finger . . .

●

76

How can you tell the gay guy in biology class?

While everyone else is dissecting frogs, he's opening flies.

●

Why didn't the masochistic little boy jack off?

His mother caught his older brother at it and said, 'If you hadn't grown so big, I'd spank you.'

●

What do you call a gay midget?

A low blow.

●

One night Fred came home from work and told his wife over dinner that he had just signed up with the company hockey team. Worried that he might hurt himself, his wife went out the next day to buy him a jockstrap.

The effeminate sales assistant was only too happy to help her. 'They come in colours, you know,' he told her. 'We have Virginal White, Ravishing Red and Promiscuous Purple.'

'I guess white will do fine,' she said.

'They come in different sizes, too, you know,' said the assistant.

'Oh, I'm really not sure what Fred's size is,' confessed his wife. So the assistant extended his index finger.

'No, it's bigger than that.'

The clerk extended a second finger alongside the first.

'No, it's bigger than that,' said the wife.

A third finger.

'Still bigger,' she said.

When the assistant stuck out his thumb too, she said, 'Yes, that's about right.'

So the assistant put all five fingers in his mouth, pulled them out, and announced expertly, 'That's a medium.'

●

What do you call a homosexual in jail?
Canned fruit.

●

What's a gay barman's favourite drink?
Fruit cocktail.

●

What do you call a faggot in the navy?
A Rear Admiral.

●

Religious

What do you call a gay nun?

A transister.

●

A little boy was throwing a temper tantrum on a crowded pavement when an elderly minister walked by. Stopping the flustered mother with an upraised hand, he bent down and whispered something in the child's ear. Instantly the child calmed, stood up, and returned docilely to his mother's side, and the bystanders burst into a smattering of applause. One took the minister by the sleeve and asked, 'Excuse me, Reverend, but what magic words *did* you use on that little boy?'

The old man smiled and gently said, 'I told him that if he didn't get the hell off the pavement, I'd kick his fucking ass to the moon.'

●

One fine day a rabbi, a minister and a priest rent a rowboat and go fishing in a nearby lake. Pretty soon the reverend says, 'If you'll excuse me, nature calls,' gets out of the boat, and walks across the water to a privy on the shore. A few minutes after he rejoins the fishing party in the same manner, the priest excuses himself for the same reason, walks across the water to the privy, and returns nice and dry to the boat. The rabbi marvels at this, wondering if they have special God-given powers, and as his own bladder fills up he wonders if he might not have some special powers himself. So he stands up and excuses himself, steps overboard, and sinks like a stone. Splashing and struggling to the surface, the rabbi yells, 'Help me, O God, help me!'

The minister and the priest look at each other, and the priest says, 'Should we tell him about the rocks?'

●

A new building was going up next door to the convent and the sisters' devotions were constantly being interrupted by the foul language used by the construction workers. Unable to stand it any longer, the Mother Superior went next door and asked to speak to the foreman. After listening to her complaint, the foreman said, 'I'm sorry, Sister, but we believe in calling a spade a spade.'

'The heck you do,' said the Mother Superior. 'You call it a fucking shovel.'

●

What do a Christmas tree and a priest have in common?

They both have balls just for decoration.

●

A nun was killing some time in the airport before her plane left so she put her penny into a weight-and-fortune machine, stood on the scales, and waited for the card to come out. It read: 'You are a Catholic nun; your height is 5' 5"; your weight is 150 lbs; and you are about to expel gas.' She couldn't believe this, but sure enough, about ten minutes later, she felt a terrific pain in her gut and had to run for the ladies' room to fart discreetly. Amazed, she returned to the machine, inserted another penny, and got a card that read: 'You are a Catholic nun, you are 5' 5"; you weigh 150 lbs; and you are going to be raped.' Sure enough, as she stepped down from the scales a man grabbed her, dragged her off to the men's room, and raped her. Staggering out of the men's room, she climbed back on the scales, inserted another penny, and got a card that read: 'You are 5' 5"; you weigh 150 lbs; and you have farted and fucked around and missed your plane.'

●

Sister Bridget was asking her third-grade class what each of them would like to be when they grew up. Little Mary said, 'I'd like to be a nurse.' Young Michael said, 'I want to be a policeman.' Little Nora said, 'I want to be a prostitute!'

Sister Bridget fainted completely away. Upon being revived, she asked again what little Nora had said, and when she was told, a smile came over her face. 'Thanks be to God,' said the sister, 'I thought she said a *Protestant.*'

●

What do you get when you cross nuns and chickens?

A pecking order.

●

A priest, a minister and a rabbi are all enjoying a beer together when a fly lands right in the priest's glass. Fishing it out, the priest shakes the beer off it and throws it in the air, saying, 'Be on your way, little creature.'

Five minutes later the fly is back, this time making a nose-dive for the minister's beer. Fishing it out and shaking it dry, the minister tosses it in the air, saying, 'Be free, little bug.'

But the fly is a slow learner and ends up five minutes later in the rabbi's glass. Picking it up and shaking it violently, the rabbi screams, 'Spit it out, spit it out!'

●

A young pastor married a girl who'd been around with lots of men while he himself had little sexual experience. On their wedding night he stepped into the bathroom to put on his pyjamas, and when he came out he was shocked to find his new wife lying nude on the bed. Alarmed, he blurted out, 'I thought I would find you on your knees by the side of the bed.'

'Nah,' she said, 'that position always gives me the hiccups.'

●

During Bible study class Freddie was much more interested in his new hot-rod car than in the lesson. His fidgeting didn't escape the Sister's notice, so she decided to give him a spot quiz. 'Who was God's son, Freddie?' she asked.

The girl behind Freddie poked him hard with her pencil and he cried out, 'Jesus!'

'Very good,' said the Sister. 'Now, who is the first member of the Holy Trinity?'

The girl poked Freddie even harder. 'God Almighty!' he blurted.

'All right,' said the Sister, deciding to throw him a trick question. 'Now tell me what Eve said to Adam their first week together.'

Once more the girl jabbed Freddie, and he screamed, 'You prick me with that one more time and I'm going to shove it up your ass!'

●

An ambitious new sales rep for Budweiser beer travelled all the way to Rome and managed to wangle an audience with the Pope himself. As soon as the two were alone together, he leaned over and whispered, 'Your Holiness, I have an offer I think might interest you. I'm in a position to give you a million pounds if you'll change the wording in the Lord's Prayer to "our daily beer". Now what do you say?'

'Absolutely not,' said the shocked Pontiff.

'OK, I understand; it's a big decision,' sympathized the salesman. 'How about five million pounds?'

'I couldn't think of it,' sputtered the Pope.

'I know it's a tough one. Tell you what – I can go up to fifty million pounds,' proposed the salesman.

Asking him to leave the room, the Pope called in the Cardinal and whispered, 'When does our contract with Mother's Pride expire?'

●

What do nuns wear on dates?

A cross-your-heart bra and no-nonsense stockings.

●

It was late at night when the nudist got a little hungry and decided to get a snack at the corner cafe. He walked in, bought a pack of chewing gum and a chocolate bar, and was heading for the door when three near-sighted nuns came in. And he was so embarrassed that he just froze.

One of the nuns walked up to him, squinted, and said, 'This must be a new vending machine.' Putting a quarter in his mouth, she pulled his dick and he stuck out the hand holding the pack of chewing gum. The second nun did the same, and got the chocolate bar.

'I do like that new vending machine,' said the first nun as they left the store. 'I got a pack of chewing gum.'

The second nun agreed. 'I got my favourite chocolate bar.'

'That's funny,' said the third nun, 'all I got was hand lotion.'

●

A priest and a rabbi were out playing golf one day when the priest looked at his watch and said, 'Pardon me, Rabbi, but I must leave to go hear confession.'

'What is this "confession?"' asked the rabbi.

'It's when I listen to my parishioners tell me their sins and I absolve them while they say a penance,' explained the priest.

'How interesting. Do you mind if I come along and watch?' asked the rabbi.

'Come on,' said the priest, and they both crowded into the priest's side of the confessional.

The first penitent, a woman, came in and said, 'Bless me, Father, for I have sinned. I have had sex with a man three times.'

'That's all right, my child,' comforted the priest. 'Put five pounds in the poor box and say three Hail Marys and you will be absolved.'

In came a second woman. 'Forgive me, Father, for I have sinned,' she said, 'because I have had intercourse with a man three times.'

'Don't worry about it,' soothed the priest. 'Put five pounds in the poor box, say five Hail Marys, and you will be absolved.'

'Hey, this looks easy,' said the rabbi. 'Do you mind if I give it a try?'

'Be my guest,' said the priest as a third woman entered the confessional. 'As long as they think it's me, they'll be forgiven.'

'Forgive me father, for I have sinned,' said the third penitent. 'I have had sex with a man two times.'

'Listen,' said the rabbi. 'Go out and do it one more time. We're having a special today – three for five quid.'

●

What does a rapist give a nun?

Unleavened head.

●

This drunk is weaving down the A21 when his reckless driving happens to come to the attention of a minister. Trying to prevent tragedy, the minister picks up speed and attempts to get ahead of the car to slow it down. But being a law-abiding citizen, the minister isn't used to speeds above 45 m.p.h. and proceeds to lose control of his car, winding up in a gully on the side of the road.

Realizing what's happened, the drunk turns around and

drives back to the wreck. 'Shay, mate, you okay?' he asks, peering in the car window.

'I'm fine, for the Lord rides with me,' retorts the minister indignantly.

'Oh yeah?' says the drunk. 'Well you better let him ride with me, 'cause you're gonna kill him.'

●

A sixteen-year-old girl went to make her confession at the neighbourhood church. Blushing slightly, she answered the priest's query: 'Well, Father, my boyfriend and I were at this party and he was kissing me, but I was innocent.' After a pause, she went on, 'Then we got into his car and he started taking my clothes off, but I was innocent, Father.' Hearing only a sceptical snort from the other side of the confessional, she continued, 'His car is a Volkswagen and I was completely undressed, so he spread my legs and put them in those two leather straps above the windows, but I was innocent, Father, I swear it.'

The priest couldn't take it any more and burst out, 'Enough of this shit. I'm the innocent here – I didn't even know what those straps were for!'

●

What's black and white and red all over?

A nun with stab wounds.

●

A six-year-old happened to be pulling his brand new wagon past the parish priest when one of the wheels came off. 'Goddammit!' cursed the kid.

'Young man,' scolded the priest severely, 'don't you ever say that again. If something goes wrong for you, say, "Help me, Lord" instead, do you understand?'

'Okay, Father,' said the kid. But the very next day a second wheel fell off just as the priest was walking by. 'Goddammit!' exploded the kid.

'What did I tell you?' boomed the priest. 'What are you supposed to say?'

'Okay, okay,' said the kid. Two days later the remaining two wheels fell off as the priest was lurking in the bushes, listening carefully. 'Help me, Lord,' said the little boy, and all four wheels jumped back on the wagon.

'Goddammit!' said the astonished priest.

•

What do you call a nun who's also a lesbian?

A nun with a bad habit.

•

One night little Johnny finished his prayers with 'God bless Grandma,' and the very next day his grandmother kicked the bucket. Johnny told his family about his prayer but no one seemed to give it too much thought. A week later he ended his prayers with, 'God bless Grandpa,' and the next day his grandfather died. The family was running a little scared by now, and when Johnny finished his prayers one night with, 'God bless Daddy,' his mother thought maybe she better warn her husband about it.

All that night Johnny's dad couldn't sleep for worrying, and the next day he came home from work early. 'I had a terrible day worrying about all this,' he confided to his wife.

'You think you had a bad day,' she said. 'The postman came to the door and dropped dead.'

•

One morning the town priest greeted one of his parishioners who was walking by holding a butterfly. 'I'm going to get some butter,' the man explained. The priest raised his eyebrows but didn't say anything, and not much later he saw the man walking home with a pound of butter under his arm.

The next day the same man passed by holding a

horsefly. 'I'm off to get myself a horse,' he said. The priest decided not to say anything, and sure enough pretty soon he saw the guy riding home on horseback.

The next day the same fellow passed by holding a pussywillow. 'Don't say a word,' said the priest. 'I'm coming with you.'

●

This fellow goes into the Catholic church. 'Bless me, Father, for I have sinned,' he says to the priest in the confessional. 'I have committed adultery.'

'I must know the name of the woman before I can grant you absolution,' says the priest. 'Was it Mrs McCaffrey, the butcher's wife?'

'No, no - and please don't ask me to reveal her name.'

'I must know. Was it Mrs O'Shaughnessy, the laundress?'

'No, it was not.'

'Then perhaps it was Mrs O'Brien from the market?'

'Certainly not,' says the man, and leaves the confessional.

'Did you get absolved?' asked the friend who'd been waiting for him outside the church.

'No,' he said, 'but I got some good leads.'

●

A rabbi and a priest were seated together on a plane. After a while, they started talking and the priest said, 'Rabbi, I hope you don't mind my asking, but I'm curious: have you ever eaten pork?'

'Actually, yes, once I got drunk and temptation overcame me. I had a ham sandwich and, I hate to admit it, I enjoyed it,' replied the rabbi. 'Now let me ask you, have you ever been with a woman?'

'Well,' responded the priest, 'I once got drunk and went to a whorehouse and purchased the services of a prostitute. I too quite enjoyed the experience.'

'It's a lot better than a ham sandwich, isn't it?'

●

Child Abuse

What's red and dances?
A baby on a burner.

●

What glows and can't scream?
A wet baby with its fingers in an electrical outlet.

●

What's blue and knocks on the window?
A baby in a fishtank.

●

Heard about the new remedy for child molesters?
Incesticides.

●

'How'd you puncture that tyre?' asked Moe.
    'Ran over a milk bottle,' explained Joe.
    'Didn't you see it?'
    'Damn kid had it hidden under his coat.'

●

What's black and blue and goes tha-dump, tha-dump?
A baby in a dryer.

●

What's black and blue and goes swish, tha-dump, tha-dump?

A baby going down an incinerator.

●

Old Age

Two elderly men sitting around the senior citizens' centre on a Sunday, catching up on each other's affairs. 'So, Herb, how's it going?' asked Larry. 'Are you getting any?'

Herb replied, 'Almost every night, I'm telling you.'

'At your age? I don't mean to be disrespectful, Herb, but I just don't believe it.'

Said Herb, 'It's true. Almost Monday night, almost Tuesday night, almost Wednesday night . . .'

●

Why is a woman over sixty like Australia?

Everyone knows it's down under, but who gives a damn?

●

An old man and his wife were sitting on their porch one warm summer afternoon, listening to a healing preacher on their favourite radio station. The preacher said, 'Now, I want you to put your hand on the part of your body that most needs some healing, and we will pray together for its return to health.' So the old woman put her hand over her heart, hoping the prayers would make it stronger. Her husband looked over slyly to make sure she wasn't looking, then snuck his hand down to his crotch. His wife looked over and said, 'Harold, the preacher said he was going to heal the part, not raise the dead!'

●

Milton was getting on in years - he was well into his eighties - and decided it was time for a last fling. So he went out and hired himself a prostitute for a last night of pleasure.

About three weeks later he felt a growing pain in his groin and rushed over to the doctor's office, insisting on an emergency consultation. The doctor examined him thoroughly, then asked if he could ask a personal question. 'Have you been with a woman any time recently?'

Milton confessed the truth.

'Well, you better go look her up right away, 'cause you're about to come!'

•

Sam and Sally were virgins when they were married and so embarrassed about the sex act that they agreed to refer to it as 'doing the laundry'. Fifty years later their prudery had not diminished, but every so often Sam would get his hopes up and ask if he could put something in the washing machine. 'Maybe in a little while, Sam,' Sally answered one cold night as they tottered into the bedroom.

Under the covers he poked her in the ribs and asked, 'How about a little laundry, honey?'

No answer from Sally, but about ten minutes later, having thought it over, she whispered, 'Okay, Sam, the washing machine's ready.'

'Aw, gee, honey,' he quavered, 'it was just a small load, I did it by hand.'

•

Did you hear about the ninety-two-year-old man who was arrested for attempted rape of a seventeen-year-old high-school girl?

The charge was 'assault with a dead weapon'.

•

This old guy and his wife have been spending the last thirty winters at the same Miami Beach resort, and for at

least twenty of them the same prostitute's been regularly
propositioning the old geezer; it's a pretty posh resort so
she figures it'd be well worth her time. Finally, tired of
fending her off after all these years, the man gives in.
'Okay,' he says, 'I'll go to bed with you. But since I retired,
my wife handles the money, so is it okay if she comes too?'

●

There was once a seventy-seven-year-old spinster who
detected something nasty going on in her nether regions
and, somewhat embarrassed, went to the doctor for tests.
Sure enough, the doctor produced a diagnosis of crabs.
'That's quite impossible,' gasped the old woman. 'I am
seventy-seven and a virgin.' Deciding to get a second
opinion, she had another doctor do a checkup, but he only
confirmed the unfortunate diagnosis. 'How can that be?'
she stammered. 'In seventy-seven years no man has ever
touched me.' And off she went to the hospital for an
enormous battery of tests. Eventually a young doctor
came into her room and announced that he had some good
news and some bad news.
      'Give me the good news first,' said the old woman.
      'You don't have crabs,' said the doctor. 'The bad news is
that your cherry has rotted and you have fruit flies.'

●

Two old ladies are sitting in their rocking-chairs at the
nursing home, reminiscing. One turns to the other and
says; 'Mildred, do you remember the minuet?'
      'Good heavens, no,' replies Mildred, 'I don't even
remember the ones I screwed.'

●

Whitney woke up in the middle of the night and cried until
his mother came in to see what was the matter. 'I have to
make pee-pee,' wailed the little boy.
      'All right,' said his mother, 'I'll take you to the
bathroom.'

'No,' insisted Whitney, 'I want Grandma.'

'Don't be silly, I can do the same thing as Grandma,' said his mother firmly.

'Huh-uh. Her hands shake.'

●

Grandpa was sitting on the front porch talking to his teenage grandson about growing old. 'Why, Teddy,' he wheezed, 'I remember going courting in the old buggy. On the way home I'd have to put my dong under a spoke in the buggy wheel to keep from peeing in my face, imagine that.'

'Yes? Go on, Grandpa,' urged Teddy.

'Well, at seventy-five things are a bit different. Now I have to rest it on one of the spokes to keep from peeing on my feet.'

●

Did you hear about the fifty-year-old hooker?

She sat down on a barstool and fell all the way to the floor.

●

Wondering what to give the older man who has everything?

A portable freezer to make it hard in an emergency.

●

This old couple are walking through the park one day when a bird flying overhead lets one drop right on the woman's head. 'Quick, dear,' she quavers, turning to her husband, 'get me some toilet paper.'

'Eh?' he says, looking at her. 'What's the use – the bird's at least a half-mile away by now.'

●

An eager-beaver young real-estate agent was doing his best to sell this old coot a condominium in Palm Beach. Having outlined its many attractions in detail, he confidently concluded his pitch: 'And, Mr Rosenblatt, this is an investment for the future.'

'Sonny,' croaked Mr Rosenblatt, 'at my age I don't even buy green bananas.'

●

The girls in the whorehouse were frankly sceptical when a ninety-year-old man came in and put his money down on the front desk, but finally a good-hearted hooker took him up to her room. Imagine her surprise when he proceeded to make love to her with more energy and skill than any man she had ever known. 'I've never come so many times,' she gasped. 'How about once more, on the house?'

'All right,' conceded the old fellow, 'but I have to take a five-minute nap and you must keep your hands on my penis, just so, while I'm asleep.' She agreed eagerly, and as soon as he woke up he gave her an even better lesson in lovemaking.

'Oh God,' gasped the whore ecstatically, 'I can't get enough of you. Please, just once more – I'll pay *you*.'

The old man agreed, subject to the same conditions, and just before he nodded off the hooker said, 'Excuse me, but would you mind explaining about the nap and why I have to keep my hands on your privates?'

'I'm ninety years old,' retorts the man, 'so is it so surprising I need a little rest? As for the other, it's because the last time while I was napping they took my wallet.'

●

The old farmer and his wife were sitting on their porch after celebrating their fiftieth wedding anniversary. At long last the wife broke the peaceful silence with a question. 'Have you ever been unfaithful to me?'

'Once, dear, just once,' quavered her husband. 'And you?'

'Just a minute,' she said and disappeared into the house, returning with a shoebox containing six kernels of corn and twenty thousand dollars in cash.

Her husband looked at her and said, 'What the hell does this mean?'

'Every time I'm unfaithful to you, I put a kernel of corn in the box,' she explained.

'Well, what's the money for?'

His wife said, 'Every time I get a bushel, I sell it.'

•

Two seventy-year-old virgins finally decide to tie the knot and to honeymoon in Miami. Once they reach the hotel suite the old woman asks, 'Well, dear, how do we do it?'

'I'm not sure, my love, but I have an idea,' answers the old gentleman. He proposed that she stand by the window and he by the door, and that they run towards each other and meet in the middle.

'That sounds wonderful, dear. I'm so proud of you,' quavers his bride, and off they go.

A little while later one of the hotel busboys says to another, 'Did you know there's an old man who fell out of the window lying naked in the middle of the pavement?'

'Yes,' answered the other busboy. 'We're still trying to get the old lady off the doorknob.'

•

Miscellaneous

A lonely woman eagerly waited for Santa to show up on Christmas Eve. When he finally scrambled out of the chimney into her living room, she asked, 'Santa, will you please stay with me?'

'Ho, ho, ho,' said Santa, 'got my presents to deliver.'

The woman took off her robe and repeated her request.

'Ho, ho, ho,' said Santa, 'gotta go, gotta go.'

The woman took off her negligée, slipped out of her panties, began to stroke her pussy, and whispered, 'Santa, won't you please stay with me?'

Santa replied, 'Ho, ho, ho, gotta stay – can't get up the chimney with my dick this way!'

•

Know how Tarzan got his famous yell?

He found Jane surrounded by a tribe of hungry cannibals. Grabbing a handy vine, he swung down to her rescue, shouting, 'Jane, grab the vine. No, Jane, the vine, the *vine* . . . Aa-aahaahaaaa!'

•

An attorney was defending his client against a charge of first-degree murder. 'Your Honour, my client is accused of stuffing his lover's mutilated body into a suitcase and heading for the Mexican border. Just north of Tijuana a cop spotted her hand sticking out of the suitcase.

'Now, I would like to stress that my client is *not* a murderer. A sloppy packer, maybe . . .'

•

After this fellow was finished at the local whorehouse, the prostitute looked up from the bed and simpered, 'What do you want to name the child?' The man thought this was a bit presumptuous and walked out, thoroughly pissed off. He came back for more a few weeks later and was even angrier when the question was asked a second time. Quickly taking off his rubber, he tied it in a knot, tossed it out the window, and said, 'If he can get out of that, I'll call him Houdini.'

•

One day a man was sunbathing on a nude beach when he noticed a little girl staring down at him, so he put a newspaper over his private parts. The girl asked him what that was, and he explained that it was his bird and that he kept it under there so it wouldn't fly away. He fell asleep, and when he woke up he found himself in a hospital room. 'What happened?' he asked.

The little girl stepped in and said, 'While you were sleeping I wanted to play with your bird. But it spat at me, so I broke its neck, crushed its eggs, and set its nest on fire.'

•

There's a rumour that some independent skin-flick producers are combining to form a major studio.

It's going to be called Twentieth-Century Fux.

•

Hear about Snow White's swingin' party?

She woke up feeling Dopey.

•

What's worse than being pissed off?

Being pissed on.

•

Jack was getting on to his commuter train when he heard a man standing on the platform yelling to a man inside the train, 'Your wife is a great fuck! Your wife is fantastic in bed!' Surprised and a little curious, Jack went over to the fellow who was doing the yelling and asked him why he'd want to say such a thing in public.

The man shrugged. 'Well, actually she's a lousy lay, but I didn't want to hurt his feelings.'

●

Bumper sticker: JOAN OF ARC IS ALIVE AND MEDIUM WELL.

●

The third-grade teacher was teaching English and repeated for her class: 'Mary had a little lamb, whose fleece was white as snow/And everywhere that Mary went, the lamb was sure to go.' She explained that this was an example of poetry, but could be changed to prose by changing the last line from 'the lamb was sure to go' to 'the lamb went with her'.

A few days later she asked for an example of poetry or prose. Johnny raised his hand and recited, 'Mary had a little pig, an ornery little runt/He stuck his nose in Mary's clothes, and smelled her little -' He stopped and asked the teacher if she wanted poetry or prose.

'Prose,' the teacher said weakly.

So Johnny said, 'Asshole.'

●

Three door-to-door vacuum-cleaner salesmen show up at a farmhouse one afternoon, and the kindly farmer agreed to buy a vacuum from each if they'll keep their hands off his virginal daughter while he's at the bank, getting the money. But when he gets back he finds all three on top of his daughter. Irate, he fires a shotgun blast over their heads, marches them out to the garden, and tells them each to pick ten of any fruit or vegetable.

The first salesman comes forward with ten peas. 'Shove them up your ass,' orders the farmer. The second guy turns up with ten tomatoes and gets the same order. He has some trouble getting them up his ass, especially as he keeps cracking up with laughter, but finally gets the job done. 'You're free to go,' the farmer says to him, 'but do you mind if I ask what's so damn funny?'

Collapsing with laughter once again, the salesman says, 'The third bloke's still out there, picking watermelons.'

●

What's a 6.9?

A 69 interrupted by a period.

●

How do you make a dead baby float?

You take your foot off its head and let it rise to the surface.

●

What's worse than finding ten dead babies in a rubbish bin?

Finding one dead baby in ten rubbish bins.

●

How did the couple into S&M have fun in their car?

They used the cigarette lighter.

●

What's Smurf sex?

Fucking till you're blue in the face.

●

When his company fell on hard times, the boss realized he'd have to lay off one of his two middle managers, although both Jack and Jill were equally honest and dedicated to their jobs. Unable to decide which to fire, the boss arbitrarily decided that the first to leave his or her desk the next morning would be the one to get the axe.

The next morning found Jill at her desk, rubbing her temples. Asking Jack for some aspirin, she headed for the water fountain and that's where the boss caught up with her. 'I've got some news for you, Jill,' he said. 'I'm going to have to lay you or Jack off.'

'Jack off,' she snapped. 'I have a headache.'

●

'Mummy, Mummy, have you seen my Cabbage Patch doll?'

'Shut up and eat your cole slaw.'

●

What do they give a cannibal who is late for dinner?

The cold shoulder.

●

A settler in the American Midwest felt he had to protect his family from wild animals and unfriendly Indians – but he also needed to chop wood for the fire. So he bought a large bell and set it up outside, instructing his wife to ring it in case of an emergency.

The next day he was busy chopping wood when he heard the bell ring in the distance. Terrified, he grabbed his rifle and ran home, only to find his wife standing in the clearing holding a tray. 'I baked you some biscuits, honey,' she said.

Patiently he explained that the bell was only for a real emergency, and went back to chopping wood. Just a few days later the bell rang again and he rushed back, only to be shown a wounded bird his son had brought home.

This, he made clear a little less patiently, was not his idea of a dangerous emergency.

A week later he rushed home at the clang of the bell. Reaching the clearing, he found that the house had been felled by a tornado, his wife had been murdered and scalped by Indians, and wildcats were gnawing the bloody remains of his children.

'Now, this is more like it!' said the settler.

●

Hear about the new combination aphrodisiac and laxative?

It's called 'Easy come, Easy go'.

●

The wife was at home when the call came from the local brewery. 'I'm afraid I have some tragic news, ma'am,' said the brewery representative. 'There's been a terrible accident: Your husband has drowned in a vat of beer.'

'Oh my God,' gasped the new widow. 'Did he . . . did he suffer much?'

'I don't think so, ma'am – he got out to pee four times before he went under.'

●

What do coffins and condoms have in common?

They both have stiffs in them, but one's coming and one's going.

●

Hear about the man who went to bed with his sister-in-law?

He had it in for his brother.

●

What would you rather be, a light bulb or a bowling ball?

Depends on whether you'd rather be screwed or fingered.

●

An angry mother took her son to the doctor and asked, 'Is a nine-year-old boy able to perform an appendectomy?'

'Of course not,' the doctor said impatiently.

The mother turned to her son and said, 'What did I tell you? Now put it back.'

●

Two strangers met on a golf course and the conversation came around to their occupations. The first man said he was in real estate: in fact he owned an apartment block that was barely visible in the distance. The second man said he was a professional assassin, but his new acquaintance was sceptical until the man took some pipes out of his golf bag and assembled them into a rifle.

'I'll be damned,' said the first guy.

'The best part of this rifle is the high-power scope,' confided the assassin, handing him the gun.

'You're right,' said the first man. 'I can see inside my own apartment with it. There's my wife . . . and she's in there with another man!' Furious, he turned to the assassin and asked how much he charged for his services, to which the reply was, 'A thousand dollars a bullet.'

The man said, 'I want to buy two bullets. I want you to kill my wife with the first one and blow that man's balls off with the second.'

Agreeing to the offer, the assassin looked through his scope and took aim. Then he lifted his head and said, 'If you'll hang on a minute, I can save you a thousand dollars.'

●

Two cannibals came upon a dead body. In order to make sure that both would get equal portions, the big cannibal said to the little cannibal, 'You start at the head and I'll start at the feet.'

Not much later the little cannibal looked up and exclaimed, 'Man, I'm having a ball.'

The big cannibal replied, 'Slow down, you're going too fast.'

What's the definition of 'hijacking?'

A masturbating astronaut.

•

It's late at night when a spaceship lands in the middle of the Yorkshire moors. The Martians - who look like your average petrol pump, not exactly, but pretty close - descend from the ship and begin looking for signs of intelligent life. Coming across a road they follow it until they come across a petrol station with one pump, which looks somewhat like a Martian - not exactly, but pretty close.

The captain is overjoyed - this must be what they are seeking! Deciding to make contact, he intones to the pump, 'Greetings. We come from planet Xjbzoldt in search of intelligent beings. Will you take us to your leader?' When there's no response, he repeats his query as loudly as possible. Still no answer, so he turns to his voice translator. Finally, enraged by the lack of a reply, he whips out his laser gun and points it at the pump. 'Why you insolent son of a whore - take us to your leader or I'll blast you!' His lieutenant tries to stop him, but it's too late. The captain fires, and an immense explosion hurls the Martians a hundred feet in the air.

Three hours later as they're coming to, the lieutenant helps the captain to his feet. In a shaky voice the captain asks, 'Wha . . . what happened?'

The lieutenant replies, 'Look, captain, if I told you once, I told you a hundred times: you just don't mess with a fellow who can wrap his prick twice around his waist and stick it in his ear.'

•

What's white and goes up?

A retarded snowflake.

A cop on the beat came across a man with his finger stuck up another man's ass. 'Hey, what's going on here?' asked the cop gruffly.

'This man had too much to drink and I'm trying to make him throw up,' was the explanation.

'Putting your finger in his asshole isn't going to do the trick,' said the cop.

'No, but when I take it out and put it in his mouth it will!'

●

Why does the crack in your ass go up and down instead of across?

So that when you're sliding downhill, you don't mumble.

●

Three travelling salesmen ran out of petrol not far from a hospitable farmer's house. He and his eighteen beautiful daughters invited them all out of the rain and said they could spend the night, although the farmer apologized for the fact that there was only one spare bedroom and two salesmen would have to sleep in the barn. The three salesmen gratefully accepted his offer, for there were no garage services available at that time of night.

The next morning the salesmen went on their way and in the car they began to compare notes about the evening's experience. 'All I thought about was straw,' said the first man, 'because I had to sleep with the horses.'

'You think that's bad,' piped up the second man. 'All I dreamed about was mud, because I was down there with the pigs. How about you, Phil?'

'I'll tell you,' said Phil blearily, 'all I could think about was golf.'

'Why golf?' asked the driver.

'Hey, if you shot eighteen holes in one night, that's all you'd be able to think about either.'

•

A prosperous stockbroker and his wife had everything money could buy, until the broker gambled on a few bad tips and lost everything. He came home with a heavy heart that night and said to his wife, 'You'd better learn to cook, Molly, so we can fire the cook.'

His wife thought it over for a few moments and said, 'Okay, but you'd better learn to screw, George, so we can fire the chauffeur.'

•

The newlyweds stopped at a farmhouse and agreed to rent a room for the night. By noon the next day they were still not up and about, so the farmer yelled up that it was last call for breakfast.

'Don't worry about us,' called the groom, 'we're living on the fruits of love.'

'Okay,' screamed the farmer, 'but stop throwing the damned skins out the window - they're choking the ducks.'

•

What does making love in a canoe have in common with light beer?

They're both fucking close to water.

•

Once there were three city boys who decided to go camping for the week. They rented a cabin up in the mountains and when they got there, one boy said, 'Who's going to cook?'

There were no volunteers so they drew straws, and the loser said, 'Okay, I'll cook. But if anyone complains, they're taking over the cooking.' Everyone agreed, and no one said a word when dinner that night was pretty terrible.

The next night the cook broiled the coffee, cindered the steak, and puked in the milk, but still no one complained.

He was pissed. The next day he came across a big pile of moose shit in the woods, came back to the cabin early, and made it into a delicious-looking pie. When his friends returned for dinner the pie was sitting in the middle of the table, and even though it smelled funny it looked great.

The greediest camper inhaled his dinner and cut himself a gigantic slice of the pie. Taking a giant bite, he opened his eyes about six inches wide and gasped, '*Moose shit* . . . but good, but good!'

●

What's the difference between a baby and a choir director?

A baby sucks his fingers . . .

●

Finally admitting he was grossly overweight, this man decided it was time to take advantage of a special introductory offer from a new weight-loss clinic in town. After handing over his payment he was shown into an empty room where he was soon joined by a gorgeous blonde. 'Hi,' she said. 'If you catch me, I'm yours.'

It took a while, but after a prolonged chase he succeeded – and was delighted to find he'd lost ten pounds in the process. After that he gave up all ideas of dieting and managed to drop ten more pounds with a brunette and eight with a redhead. But he was still fifty pounds overweight, so he decided to sign up for the clinic's more drastic programme. He was waiting eagerly in an empty room when the door opened and in came a twenty-stone gay leper who grinned and said, 'If I catch you, you're mine!'

●

What's 71?

Sixty-nine with two fingers up your ass.

106

What's 72?

Sixty-nine with three people watching.

●

This man called up his lawyer to tell him he was suing for divorce, and the lawyer enquired as to his grounds for the suit.

'Can you believe it, my wife says I'm a lousy lover?' sputtered the husband.

'*That's* why you're suing?' asked the lawyer.

'Of course not. I'm suing because she knows the difference.'

●

One night Judge O'Brien tottered into his house very late and very drunk indeed, so bombed that he had managed to throw up all over himself. In the morning he sheepishly told his wife that a drunk sitting next to him on the train home had managed to vomit all over him.

The judge managed to make it in to the courthouse, where it occurred to him that his story might not be truly convincing to his wife. Inspired, he called home and said, 'Darling, you won't believe this but I've just had the drunk who threw up on me last night show up in court, and I gave him thirty days.'

'Give him sixty days,' said the judge's wife. 'He shit in your trousers too.'

●

A middle-aged man confided to his doctor that he was tired of his wife and wished there was some way of doing her in so that he could have some good years left to himself. 'Screw her every day for a year,' counselled the doctor. 'She'll never make it.'

As chance would have it, it was about a year later when the doctor happened to drop by his patient's house. On the porch sat the husband looking frail and thin. Tan and robust, his wife could be seen out at the back splitting wood.

107

'Well, Sam, you're looking good,' said the doctor uneasily, 'and Laura certainly is the picture of health.'

'Little does she know,' hissed Sam with a wicked little smile, 'she dies tomorrow.'

●

Help bring some love into the world:

Fuck someone today!

●

It's after dinner when this fellow realizes he's out of cigarettes. He decides to pop down to the pub for a pack, telling his wife he'll be right back. The barman offers him a pint on the house and he decides he has time for just one. He's nursing it along when a gorgeous blonde comes in the door, but he looks the other way because he knows he has no time to fool around. So can he help it if she comes and sits right next to him and says how thirsty she is?

One thing leads to another and eventually the girl says how much she likes him and invites him back to her apartment to get better acquainted. How can he refuse? They go back to her place and go at it like crazy, and the next thing he knows it's four o'clock in the morning. Jumping out of bed, the man shakes the girl awake and asks if she has any baby powder.

'Yes, in the bathroom cabinet,' she says groggily.

He dusts his hands liberally with the powder, drives home at 90 m.p.h., and pulls into the driveway to find his wife waiting up for him with a rolling pin in her hand. 'So where've you been?' she screeches.

'Well, you see, darling,' he stammers. 'I only went out for cigarettes, but Jake offered me a beer and then this beautiful bombshell walked in and we got talking and drinking and we've been back at her flat, fucking like bunnies . . .'

'Wait a minute,' snaps his wife. 'Let me see your hands.' Turning on him furiously, she says, 'Don't you *ever* try lying to me again, you rotten little skunk. You've been bowling again!'

What's worse than Jimmy Durante with a bloody nose?

Dolly Parton with breast cancer.

•

There is a young woman who, instead of disposing of her tampons normally, throws them into her wardrobe. One day she is entertaining her lover when she hears the front door open, so she quickly hides him in the wardrobe and locks the door. It's her husband surprising her with two tickets for a weekend in Hawaii, and in her excitement she forgets all about her lover and dashes off to Hawaii. On Monday she waits till her husband has gone off to work and opens the wardrobe door, expecting the worse. But he's in fine shape and says cheerfully, 'Hell, if it wasn't for all those jam doughnuts you had in there, I never would have made it!'

•

Two old tramps are walking along the railway tracks, starving, because they haven't eaten in three days. Coming across a dead and mangled cat, the first tramp says, 'Oh boy – lunch!' He digs in, stopping only to ask his friend if he wants some. 'No, thanks, I think I'll pass,' is the answer. So the first tramp devours the whole cat, leaving nothing behind but fur and bones, and they continue their walk down the tracks. About a mile later the first tramp turns green and throws up the whole cat. All excited, his companion says happily, 'That's what I've been waiting for – a hot lunch!'

•

What's grosser than gross?

Two vampires fighting over a used tampon.

•

What the difference between rude and crude?

Rude is when you throw your underwear against the wall and crude is when it sticks.

●

After a long and difficult delivery, the obstetrician finally pulled the baby out, whirled it around over his head, and let go so that it splattered all over the wall. 'Doctor!' shrieked the woman. 'That was my baby!'
  'That's okay. It was dead anyhow.'

●

The victim of an awful automobile accident was pronounced dead on arrival at the hospital, and the emergency-room nurse was instructed to prepare the body for the undertaker. Removing his bloody clothes, she discovered that the young man had died with the most massive erection she had ever seen. Unable to take her eyes off it, she finally yielded to temptation, took off her panties, straddled the stiff, and proceeded to enjoy herself. She was getting down from the table when a second nurse came in and reprimanded her for her obscene behaviour. 'What's the harm?' shot back the first nurse. 'I enjoyed it, and he surely didn't mind it. Besides, he can't complain and I can't get pregnant. Why don't you give it a try.'
  'Oh, I couldn't possibly,' said the second nurse, blushing. 'First, he's dead, and second, I've got my period. Listen, the doctor wants you in the operating room, and I'm supposed to finish up in here.' She got to work but soon found herself terribly excited by this massive hard-on and climbed on top of it. Just as she was starting to come, she was astonished to feel the man climax too. Looking down and seeing his eyelids starting to flutter, she exclaimed, 'I thought you were dead!'
  'I thought I was, too, lady,' said the man, 'until you gave me that blood transfusion.'

●

How can you tell if a fence is electrified?

Throw a puppy at it and see if he gets fried.

●

What's worse than your dentist telling you you have herpes?

Your mother telling you.

●

Did you hear about the Irish fellow who ate pussy?

He spat out the kittens after he was done.

●

What's grosser than a thousand dead babies in a pile?

One eating its way out.

What's even grosser?

When it goes back for seconds.

●

A young baseball pitcher was taking a few warm-up tosses from the mound when he noticed a beautiful brunette in the stands right in front of him with her legs spread wide. The pitcher could see a dark patch between her legs and began to wonder if the patch was her pussy or her panties. The game started and by the second inning the pitcher was dying to know. Calling his catcher up to the mound, he said, 'Say, man, there's this chick right behind you that has her legs wide open. Go up there and let me know if it's pussy or underwear.'

The catcher went up eagerly into the stands, but when he came back he was puking his guts out and was taken off to the showers. Now the pitcher was really curious. At the bottom of the fifth he couldn't stand it any longer. Calling the shortstop over for a conference, he explained about the girl. 'I'm going nuts, Bobby, I've got to know whether it's pussy or panties. Will you check it out for me?'

The shortstop was more than willing. He took a quick time-out to run up into the stands, only to stagger back down white as a sheet, retching violently.

By the ninth inning the pitcher's curiosity was still unsatisfied, and he hit on a really reliable person, his manager. 'Stan, I've had this problem the whole game,' he said, explaining the situation. 'Is it black panties or pussy?'

'Be right back,' said his manager confidently. But he too was puking and pale as he stumbled back down to the field. He was heading for the showers when the pitcher simply couldn't stand it any more. Abandoning the mound, he ran over screaming desperately, 'What is it? What is it? Pussy or underwear?'

The manager looked at him weakly. 'Flies,' he said.